Paranormal Phenomena

Norah Piehl, *Book Editor*

GREENHAVEN PRESS

A part of Gale, Cengage Learning

GALE
CENGAGE Learning™

Detroit • New York • San Francisco • New Haven, Conn • Waterville, Maine • London

Elizabeth Des Chenes, *Managing Editor*

© 2012 Greenhaven Press, a part of Gale, Cengage Learning

Gale and Greenhaven Press are registered trademarks used herein under license.

For more information, contact:
Greenhaven Press
27500 Drake Rd.
Farmington Hills, MI 48331-3535
Or you can visit our Internet site at gale.cengage.com

For product information and technology assistance, contact us at

Gale Customer Support, 1-800-877-4253
For permission to use material from this text or product, submit all requests online at www.cengage.com/permissions

Further permissions questions can be e-mailed to permissionrequest@cengage.com

Articles in Greenhaven Press anthologies are often edited for length to meet page requirements. In addition, original titles of these works are changed to clearly present the main thesis and to explicitly indicate the author's opinion. Every effort is made to ensure that Greenhaven Press accurately reflects the original intent of the authors. Every effort has been made to trace the owners of copyrighted material.

Cover image © marema/Shutterstock.com.

LIBRARY OF CONGRESS CATALOGING-IN-PUBLICATION DATA

Paranormal phenomena / Norah Piehl, book editor.
    p. cm. -- (Introducing issues with opposing viewpoints)
  Includes bibliographical references and index.
  ISBN 978-0-7377-5684-5 (hardcover)
 1. Parapsychology. I. Piehl, Norah
  BF1031.P3318 2011
  130--dc22
                                           2011015609

Printed in the United States of America
1 2 3 4 5 6 7 15 14 13 12 11

Contents

Chapter 3: Does Belief in Paranormal Phenomena Conflict with Religious Beliefs?

I ndulging in a wide spectrum of ideas, beliefs, and perspectives is a critical cornerstone of democracy. After all, it is often debates over differences of opinion, such as whether to legalize abortion, how to treat prisoners, or when to enact the death penalty, that shape our society and drive it forward. Such diversity of thought is frequently regarded as the hallmark of a healthy and civilized culture. As the Reverend Clifford Schutjer of the First Congregational Church in Mansfield, Ohio, declared in a 2001 sermon, "Surrounding oneself with only like-minded people, restricting what we listen to or read only to what we find agreeable is irresponsible. Refusing to entertain doubts once we make up our minds is a subtle but deadly form of arrogance." With this advice in mind, Introducing Issues with Opposing Viewpoints books aim to open readers' minds to the critically divergent views that comprise our world's most important debates.

Introducing Issues with Opposing Viewpoints simplifies for students the enormous and often overwhelming mass of material now available via print and electronic media. Collected in every volume is an array of opinions that captures the essence of a particular controversy or topic. Introducing Issues with Opposing Viewpoints books embody the spirit of nineteenth-century journalist Charles A. Dana's axiom: "Fight for your opinions, but do not believe that they contain the whole truth, or the only truth." Absorbing such contrasting opinions teaches students to analyze the strength of an argument and compare it to its opposition. From this process readers can inform and strengthen their own opinions, or be exposed to new information that will change their minds. Introducing Issues with Opposing Viewpoints is a mosaic of different voices. The authors are statesmen, pundits, academics, journalists, corporations, and ordinary people who have felt compelled to share their experiences and ideas in a public forum. Their words have been collected from newspapers, journals, books, speeches, interviews, and the Internet, the fastest growing body of opinionated material in the world.

Introducing Issues with Opposing Viewpoints shares many of the well-known features of its critically acclaimed parent series, Opposing Viewpoints. The articles are presented in a pro/con format, allowing readers to absorb divergent perspectives side by side. Active reading questions preface each viewpoint, requiring the student to approach the material thoughtfully and carefully. Useful charts, graphs, and cartoons supplement each article. A thorough introduction provides readers with crucial background on an issue. An annotated bibliography points the reader toward articles, books, and websites that contain additional information on the topic. An appendix of organizations to contact contains a wide variety of charities, nonprofit organizations, political groups, and private enterprises that each hold a position on the issue at hand. Finally, a comprehensive index allows readers to locate content quickly and efficiently.

Introducing Issues with Opposing Viewpoints is also significantly different from Opposing Viewpoints. As the series title implies, its presentation will help introduce students to the concept of opposing viewpoints and learn to use this material to aid in critical writing and debate. The series' four-color, accessible format makes the books attractive and inviting to readers of all levels. In addition, each viewpoint has been carefully edited to maximize a reader's understanding of the content. Short but thorough viewpoints capture the essence of an argument. A substantial, thought-provoking essay question placed at the end of each viewpoint asks the student to further investigate the issues raised in the viewpoint, compare and contrast two authors' arguments, or consider how one might go about forming an opinion on the topic at hand. Each viewpoint contains sidebars that include at-a-glance information and handy statistics. A Facts About section located in the back of the book further supplies students with relevant facts and figures.

Following in the tradition of the Opposing Viewpoints series, Greenhaven Press continues to provide readers with invaluable exposure to the controversial issues that shape our world. As John Stuart Mill once wrote: "The only way in which a human being can make some approach to knowing the whole of a subject is by hearing what can be said about it by persons of every variety of opinion and studying all modes in which it can be looked at by every character of mind. No wise man ever acquired his wisdom in any mode but this." It is to this principle that Introducing Issues with Opposing Viewpoints books are dedicated.

Introduction

During the 2010 Soccer World Cup tournament, one unlikely star emerged, and he was not a striker for Germany or the goalkeeper for Spain. This celebrity, known only as "Paul," beat oddsmakers to correctly predict the outcome of each of the German team's matches, including the final against Spain. But Paul was not a soccer insider or an expert on the game. He was not even human. Paul was an octopus, and from his tank in a German aquarium, he chose between two food boxes, each containing an identical mussel and each marked with an opposing team's country flag.

The accuracy of Paul's predictions became a sensation during the soccer tournament. But was Paul, known by some as the "oracle octopus," psychic? Or could random chance account for his remarkable winning streak? Most skeptics would argue for the latter, but animal fanciers might beg to differ. In a 2010 Associated Press poll, 43 percent of pet owners claimed to believe their pets have psychic abilities.

Some of the extraordinary powers attributed to pets include sensing approaching serious storms, earthquakes, or other impending disasters; predicting their owners' catastrophic health incidents such as seizures or strokes; or even seeming to know, when their owners are still miles away, that they are on their way home. Biologist Rupert Sheldrake has collected extensive anecdotes about pets who seem to have extraordinary, even psychic, connections to humans. In his book *Dogs That Know When Their Owners Are Coming Home*, he tells, for example, the story of Whiskins, a cat that belongs to a college professor and his wife. The wife always knows when her husband calls on the phone because Whiskins paws at the receiver, sometimes even knocking it to the ground. "If someone else telephones, Whiskins takes no notice," the woman says.

Sheldrake argues that anecdotes like this one point to a whole field of animals' paranormal abilities—particularly in pets—that science has, to date, failed to investigate. But that has not stopped pet owners, animal lovers, and others from probing animals' telepathy, uncanny predictions, remarkable sense of direction, and other apparently paranormal abilities. Because of people's close emotional bonds with their pets, the idea of being able to communicate mind-to-mind with pets seems particularly appealing. TV's Animal Planet network aired a program called *The Pet Psychic* from 2002 to 2003, starring "animal communicator" Sonya Fitzpatrick. Books such as *Is Your Pet Psychic?* and *The Complete Idiot's Guide to Pet Psychic Communication* offer pet owners step-by-step instructions on establishing telepathic communication with animals.

Skeptics, however, argue that what pet owners might interpret as their pet's mind-reading abilities—the dog that runs to the back door moments after his owner considers the possibility of a walk, the cat that curls up and goes to sleep as soon as her owner reaches the last page of her bedtime book chapter—are actually explainable by subtle cues of body language or routines that are subconscious to humans but readily apparent to their pets. The dog owner might, for example, think about taking his dog for walk at approximately the same time every day. The cat owner might adjust her position slightly when she realizes she is on the last page of her chapter.

But what about tales of animals with extraordinary powers of prediction? Besides Paul the Octopus, one of the most notable recent examples was Oscar, a resident cat in a Rhode Island nursing home who became famous for curling up on the beds of patients who died shortly thereafter. According to the nursing home doctor who has written about Oscar's affection for the terminally ill, Oscar has correctly predicted the impending deaths of more than fifty patients over the course of several years. Believers point to Oscar's tendency as an indication of animals' extreme compassion and uncanny perception.

Skeptics might argue, instead, that Oscar was living at a nursing home, after all, an environment in which many people die every week, making Oscar's odds pretty good. No one ever did a systematic study of Oscar's overall behavior to see if Oscar also curled up regularly next to patients who did *not* die shortly after. It is not surprising that doctors and nurses remember Oscar's connection to patients who died, especially once they started to identify a pattern. Robert T. Carroll of the *Skeptic's Dictionary* suggests, though, "Before I'd look for an explanation for Oscar's behavior, I'd require a more formal method of observation than just relying on the memories of Dr. Dosa and his staff."

History is filled with examples of animals—psychic geese, fortune-telling pigs, a mind-reading horse named Clever Hans—whose abilities were later shown to be elaborate hoaxes, the result of specialized training rather than paranormal powers. But, as Sheldrake points out, the field of human-animal psychic connections has never been adequately examined using modern scientific techniques and tools. Perhaps science will confirm pets' extraordinary abilities; perhaps it will uncover other explanations that underlie these fascinating anecdotes. But one fact remains—whether psychic or not, people cherish a unique emotional connection with the animals in their lives.

Chapter 1

Do Paranormal Phenomena Exist?

A magician holds a Zenner card. Zenner cards were first used to test alleged ESP candidates, but magicians use them today for magic tricks.

Anecdotal Evidence Supports the Existence of ESP

Wesley J. Smith

> *"But there is plenty of anecdotal evidence for ESP. For example, over the years, I have had a few dreams come precisely true."*

In the following viewpoint Wesley J. Smith discusses the controversy likely to ensue over the scientific evidence for extrasensory perception (ESP) presented in a paper that was to be published by Cornell professor emeritus Daryl J. Bem in the respected *Journal of Personality and Social Psychology*. Smith discusses his own belief in ESP, asserting that there is much anecdotal evidence of the phenomenon. He also relates an anecdote about a dream he had that came true. Most modern scientists would not regard his experience as valid evidence for ESP, but Smith is hopeful that Bem's work will lend credence to his contention his own dream came true.

Smith is an attorney, an award-winning author, and a senior fellow at the Discovery Institute's Center on Human Exceptionalism. In 2004 the *National Journal* named him as one of the nation's top expert thinkers in bioengineering.

AS YOU READ, CONSIDER THE FOLLOWING QUESTIONS:
  1. Why does Smith say that results of Daryl J. Bem's paper will be resisted at all costs?
  2. How do the details of author Smith's dream compare with the actual events?
  3. According to the author, how would a scientist explain Smith's dream and accident?

Oh my, the fur is going to fly on this one. The NYT [*New York Times*] is reporting that "one of psychology's most respected journals," *The Journal of Personality and Social Psychology*, will publish a paper validating the existence of extra sensory perception [ESP].

From the story:

> One of psychology's most respected journals has agreed to publish a paper presenting what its author describes as strong evidence for extrasensory perception, the ability to sense future events. The paper describes nine unusual lab experiments performed over the past decade by its author, Daryl J. Bem, an emeritus professor at Cornell [University], testing the ability of college students to accurately sense random events, like whether a computer program will flash a photograph on the left or right side of its screen. The studies include more than 1,000 subjects. . . .

This paper's conclusions will be resisted at all costs because if it is true, it would challenge the purely materialistic paradigm which scientists insist must not be strayed from in explaining observable phenomena.

I believe that random ESP happens, but I don't think it can be proved scientifically—precisely because it isn't testable or falsifiable. And, if it happens, I don't think it is something we control, making it even less subject to scientific study.

But there is plenty of anecdotal evidence for ESP. For example, over the years, I have had a few dreams come precisely true. The one I am about to relate, I have no doubt, happened just as I will describe it. Indeed, it was so startling, I remember the details forty-plus years later. This was a year or two after I graduated from high school:

At the start, people were chasing each other in speed boats. Then, as dreams go, I was suddenly sitting on a low wall by the Alhambra High School gym. I was with my best friend, Rick. We were sitting next to each other, but sitting further apart than our usual social space custom. That seemed a bit odd. My head hurt. I put my hand to where it hurt and there was a little blood. I had a plain brown paper bag in my hand and I started to rip it apart, not in a furious way, but as if I was (what we used to call) spaced. This tearing revealed a paperback book, the name of which I no longer recall, but was pretty big at the time because the movie had starred (as I recall) Jane Fonda.

End of dream. It seemed so odd to me that I would be at my old high school. But I quickly forgot about it.

A short time later, I went with Rick to the movies. Before the movie, I bought a paperback book. This was still the day of the double feature. The first movie came and went. The second movie was not good. We began to talk about leaving. Then, there was a scene of

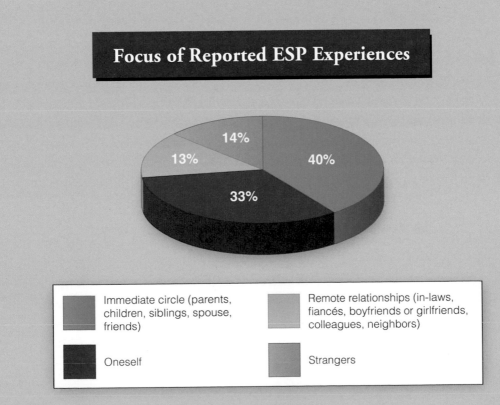

Focus of Reported ESP Experiences

14%
13%
40%
33%

Immediate circle (parents, children, siblings, spouse, friends)

Remote relationships (in-laws, fiancés, boyfriends or girlfriends, colleagues, neighbors)

Oneself

Strangers

Taken from: Sally Rhine Feather, *The Gift*. New York: St. Martin's, 2005, p. 37.

people chasing each other in speed boats. I didn't remember my dream, but sure had that old *déjà vu*.

We walked out of the movie right after that scene and decided to go to our restaurant hangout. This took us by our old high school. I usually drove, and Rick often changed my car's radio buttons so they all went to the same station. He thought it was funny. He drove this particular evening because he had purchased his first car, a used Mustang, of which he was quite proud. So, I returned the favor and altered the buttons so they all played the same station. As we drove by our old school, he tried to change the channel. "What the (expletive deleted)", he said, and he took his eye off the road. BAM! We crashed into a phone pole. I hit my head on the padded dash, but not too hard because the lap seat belt (thank you, Ralph Nader!) caught me and kept me from going through the windshield.

We were shaken, but not seriously hurt. Rick's car was wrecked. We went to a phone booth by the high school gym and called my dad to come help us. We were sitting on a short wall waiting for him to come. I began to get that *Twilight Zone* feeling when I noticed we were sitting an odd distance from each other. My head hurt. I felt the spot and there was blood on my hand. I then had the odd feeling I had lived this before and began to absent mindedly tear the paper bag. When I saw the name of the book my heart leaped into my throat! My dream came back in a flash. And I told Rick that I had dreamed it before. (He wasn't amused.) Interestingly, I didn't dream (or didn't remember) the *cause* of our being at the high school, sitting on the wall. Only the aftermath. (So what good was it? Who knows? I am just reporting the facts.)

The above really happened, with the only potentially false memory being whether the book had been made into a movie starring Jane Fonda. But to a scientist, it didn't really happen, or it is faulty memory, or I somehow took a less specific dream and added the details after the event. Whatever.

But if ESP is real, then I could well have had a dream that came true in very specific details. And it could well mean that human capacities—or existence—is far greater than anything understood—or accepted—in the philosophy of science.

So, there will be major push-back—which the *Times* notes, has already begun. Some of it will be proper science–criticizing methods and conclusions. And they may well be right. I don't have a dog in that fight. But the *zeal* that underlies the coming attacks will be about something far more encompassing than the usual scientific scrimmages. It will be about a threatened world view.

EVALUATING THE AUTHOR'S ARGUMENTS:

Wesley J. Smith, the author of this viewpoint, contrasts his own anecdotal dream and accident experience with the materialistic paradigm and philosophy of science. Can either worldview prove its case or disprove the opposing worldview? Explain, using evidence from the viewpoint.

A Scientific Experiment Disproves the Existence of ESP

Jessica R. Henderson

"We're hard-wired to see patterns in things that are probably random."

Although parapsychology researchers started out by using cards and dice to prove (or disprove) psychic phenomena, modern technology gives researchers many new tools to use as they investigate the existence of extrasensory perception (ESP). According to Jessica R. Henderson, psychology researchers at Harvard University used functional magnetic resonance imaging to look at brain activity patterns while subjects looked at photographs presented directly and via ESP-type stimuli. They discovered that participants' brains responded identically to both types of stimuli and suggested that this casts doubt on the existence of ESP.

Henderson was an English major at Harvard University, from which she graduated in 2011. She was an associate arts editor for *The Harvard Crimson*.

H arvard psychologists have released a study that they say provides the most convincing evidence yet against the existence of extrasensory perception (ESP).

In a study published in this month's [January 2008] issue of the *Journal of Cognitive Neuroscience*, graduate student Samuel T. Moulton '01 and Psychology Professor Stephen M. Kosslyn used functional magnetic resonance imaging (fMRI) to assess whether

A subject participating in extrasensory perception research is given a test. The image on the subject's forehead represents his correct prediction of the symbol on the card.

individuals can have knowledge that does not come from normal perceptual processes. This focus on the brain sets their study apart from previous ESP research.

In the study, researchers tested three types of ESP: telepathy, clairvoyance, and precognition.

The procedure involved participants viewing sets of photographs while inside an fMRI scanner. Some of the pictures, designated "ESP stimuli," were also presented to the subject via the different forms of ESP. Stimuli shown telepathically were presented simultaneously to another person—the subject's relative, romantic partner or friend—in a separate location. Stimuli presented by clairvoyance, the ability to perceive distant things or events, were displayed on a computer located outside the subject's field of vision. Finally, pictures presented through precognition, the ability to see into the future, were shown to subjects at a later time.

A "Null Result"

According to Moulton, if ESP existed, the brain would respond differently to pictures designated as ESP stimuli and non-ESP stimuli. Theoretically, pictures perceived through ESP should produce a pattern in the brain similar to ones produced when an individual sees a previously encountered stimulus.

Instead, Moulton found that participants responded identically to both stimuli types, resulting in the lack of a statistically significant difference that is referred to as a "null result."

Moulton said null results have made previous ESP research difficult to interpret, but that he wanted to design an experiment that would give information independent of whether or not it produced null results.

"We didn't find anything, but we didn't find anything in an interesting way," he said.

"ESP Pizza: You'll get it before you order it or it's free!," cartoon by Roy Delgado, www.cartoonStock.com. Copyright © Roy Delgado. Reproduction rights obtainable from www.CartoonStock.com.

Moulton said he was initially inspired by research he conducted for his senior thesis, which demonstrated that brain activity is affected by previous exposure, even when this exposure is subconscious.

No Conclusive Proof

When asked why people believe in ESP, Moulton said he believes that cognitive biases can result in people interpreting events in a paranormal way.

"We're hard-wired to see patterns in things that are probably random," he said.

He acknowledged that while null results can never be used to conclusively prove that ESP does not exist, he was glad to have done his part toward settling the age-old debate.

Aside from getting published, Kosslyn said that the study also provided him with a Christmas present to give.

"I got my mom's brain on the cover of the journal," Moulton said. "She participated in the study, and then they put her scan on the cover, and that was her present."

EVALUATING THE AUTHOR'S ARGUMENTS:

Jessica R. Henderson describes the "null result" obtained in an ESP experiment performed by two Harvard psychologists. Do you think this result disproves the existence of ESP? Explain your answer.

Virtual Reality Can Simulate an Out-of-Body Experience

Valentine Low

An out-of-body experience is the sensation or perception of standing outside one's own body. According to Valentine Low, scientists at a Swedish university have been able to trigger this sensation through the use of virtual-reality goggles that give subjects the sensation that not only are they outside of their own bodies, they are actually inhabiting someone else's. As this account of the experiment describes, these perceptions can be extremely vivid and lifelike, even when the subject is consciously aware of the experiment's methods and outcomes.

Low is a staff writer for *The Times* (UK) newspaper. Prior to writing for *The Times*, he worked at *The London Evening Standard*.

> *"As far as I can tell I am feeling quite well— although I have to admit that I am not feeling myself."*

AS YOU READ, CONSIDER THE FOLLOWING QUESTIONS:
1. As stated by the author, what are some potential applications of this research?
2. As described by Low, who is "François"?
3. How does the writer react when the researcher appears to pull a knife across his (virtual) stomach?

I am standing in a plain, blue-curtained room in Stockholm having an out-of-body experience. In the space of a few minutes I am a 30-year-old female PhD student with dark hair and glasses and a shop dummy called François.

I think to myself: people normally have to take psychedelic drugs to induce this sort of effect. Either that, or suffer a near-death experience, and as far as I can tell I am feeling quite well—although I have to admit that I am not feeling myself. It is all very disturbing, and most disturbing of all when they threaten me with a knife; but more of that later.

FAST FACT

Researchers have used magnet-studded helmets to generate the sensation of floating outside the body.

My experience of not being myself has come courtesy of scientists at the Karolinska Institute, where they have devised an experiment to convince people that they inhabit a body other than their own.

An attempt to understand how people perceive their own bodies, the research has a range of potential applications, from improving robotics to the design of prosthetic limbs. It could also help psychiatric patients with a disturbed sense of self, including those with anorexia and bulimia, or even be used for confronting racial and sexual prejudice.

Normally the institute does the experiment with people who don't know what is coming—"naive subjects". I, however, have read about their work already and know what is going to happen, so the question is: can my mind be fooled into thinking that my body is not my own?

The experiment works like this. Special goggles are attached to my head, with small screens inside the eyepieces. Meanwhile, Valeria Petkova, the PhD student who is carrying out the research under the supervision of Henrik Ehrsson, is standing in front of me wearing a headpiece with a pair of cameras on top.

The picture from the cameras, which are pointing at me, is relayed via a wire to my goggles, which means that I see a stereoscopic image of myself from the point of view of someone standing in front of me. I look at this man in a blue suit and think: "He looks just like the bloke I saw in the mirror this morning." But he is nothing to do with me."

Then we shake hands; or rather, clasp hands and squeeze them rhythmically in time with a metronome. What it does to my head is very, very unsettling. I can see this hand where my hand normally is, and every time my brain says "squeeze", I can see it squeezing the

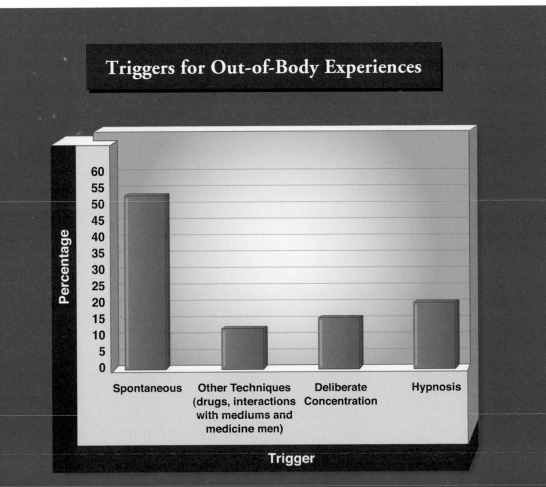

Triggers for Out-of-Body Experiences

Researchers use virtual reality experiments to trigger the sensation of out-of-body experiences.

hand opposite, the one belonging to the bloke in the blue suit. That thumb pressing down on the man's hand—that's my thumb, surely? And those tendons in the wrist that I can see tensing—they are my tendons, aren't they?

That is what my brain is telling me, anyway. But it is not my thumb, they are not my tendons: they are Valeria's, and the last time I checked I was a male British journalist from Shepherds Bush in West London, not a neuroscience PhD student from Bulgaria.

Having had my fill of being Ms Petkova, I get to have a go at being François. He is a 6ft mannequin with a rippling torso, and a helmet on his head with twin cameras attached; part male demigod, part complete dork. This time the cameras are pointing down so that François is looking down his well-toned torso at his toes, and that is the image that I see in my goggles.

I look down at my toes too, with the result that what I see is not the familiar and frankly rather depressing sight of my less-than-perfect torso, but the mannequin's impressive six-pack. It makes a pleasant change—although I cannot help noticing that François is somewhat lacking in the trouser department.

Ms Petkova takes a couple of pens, and simultaneously strokes my torso with one pen and the dummy's with the other. That is not what I see in my goggles, however: all I see is the pen stroking the dummy's torso, while I can feel the other pen stroking mine. What my brain tells me is that I can feel that pen stroking that rippling six-pack—even though intellectually I know that it is not.

Suddenly, she is drawing a knife across my stomach, and I give an involuntary gasp of shock. Half a second later I feel a complete fool, because not only did Ms Petkova warn me that she was going to produce the knife but I know that it was nowhere near my stomach, it was on the dummy's. It just looked like where my stomach should be, and my brain reacted accordingly.

They all get fooled, apparently. In another experiment, an assistant draws the knife across the subject's wrist while they clasp hands with Ms Petkova, while electrodes on the skin measure the body's autonomic fear response. If he draws it across the subject's wrist—not quite touching—but the subject thinks it is Ms Petkova's wrist, then the body does not react; if he draws it across hers, but the subject thinks it is his or her own, then the body reacts as if it is under attack.

So perhaps I should not feel too much of a wimp. Anyway, it wasn't really me, it was just a man who looked like me. I wasn't even there.

EVALUATING THE AUTHOR'S ARGUMENTS:

In the following viewpoint Jaime T. Licauco criticizes scientists who take a neurological or physiological approach to understanding paranormal phenomena such as out-of-body experiences. What responses do you think he would have to the experiment described in this viewpoint by Valentine Low?

Paranormal Phenomena Are Not Simply Neurological Disorders

"Because science has no knowledge of the astral body, its characteristics or powers, it creates a model based merely on physiological and neurological evidence."

Jaime T. Licauco

One of the definitions of paranormal phenomena is that they defy reason, logic, or science. This definition becomes problematic as new scientific methods, such as those described in the previous viewpoint, allow researchers to document or even replicate these phenomena in the lab. Some believers in the paranormal suggest that this clinical approach to studying these phenomena overlooks the complexities and variation involved in paranormal experiences. Here, Jaime T. Licauco offers several anecdotes to illustrate how, in his view, scientific research in this area is perhaps too limited in its approach and simplistic in its conclusions.

Licauco is a Filipino parapsychologist and management consultant. He is the founder of the Inner Mind Development Institute, a training center devoted to the study of paranormal phenomena. His books include *Beyond Ordinary Reality: Exploring the Powers of Your Inner Mind* and *True Encounters with the Unknown: The Psychic, the Mystical and the Strange.*

AS YOU READ, CONSIDER THE FOLLOWING QUESTIONS:
1. According to a Swiss researcher cited by the author, what percentage of people have had out-of-body experiences?
2. What does the author say is the scientific theory on why certain native peoples can walk on hot coals?
3. According to Licauco, what is the defining difference between the experience of the experimental pilots and those who undergo actual near-death experiences?

How does science look at the phenomenon of out-of-body experience (OOBE) or astral projection?

My Australian friend, Donald McDowall, a well-known chiropractor and psychic researcher from Australia who is married to a Filipina clairvoyant [psychic], Annie, gave me a copy of an article from the Internet explaining OOBE from a neurological standpoint.

The article (*OOBE and their Neural Basis*) began with a description of a typical out-of-body experience:

"I was in bed and about to fall asleep when I had the distinct impression that I was at the ceiling level looking down at my body on the bed. I was very startled and frightened; immediately (afterwards) I felt that I was consciously back in the (body on the) bed again."

The author, Professor Olaf Blanke of the Laboratory of Cognitive Neuroscience in a Swiss University, says "recent neurological evidence shows that these experiences are related to an interference with the temporo-parietal junction of the brain." This is the part of the brain that gives a person a sense of selfhood.

Ten Percent of the Population Experience OOBE

Blanke says OOBE occurs in about 10 percent of the population, most of the world's cultures and several medical conditions.

I wonder how he arrived at the 10 percent figure. I would assume the majority of people have such experiences. However, many are reluctant to tell their stories.

Blanke adds: "Some clinicians have observed OOBE in association with various neurological conditions, but mainly in epileptic seizures and migraine. These early reports have also allowed us to link OOBE with deficient visual, vestibular [relating to balance], and multi-sensory processing."

Notice how scientists regard OOBE as not normal. They suggest sickness.

Blanke says: "On the basis of these findings, our team proposed a cognitive model for OOBE relating them to failure of integration of proprioceptive [stimuli produced within an organism], tactile, [touch] and visual information of one's body (personal space)."

Let me try to say this in simple language. In a normal state, we know exactly where we are in relation to our body and surroundings. We sense ourselves as being inside our physical body.

When we think or sense ourselves to be out of our body, that is because there is an interference or anomaly [abnormality] in our sense of where we are in relation to our surrounding. We seem to think we

Research at the Swiss Laboratory of Cognitive Neuroscience indicates that approximately 10 percent of the population undergo out-of-body experiences.

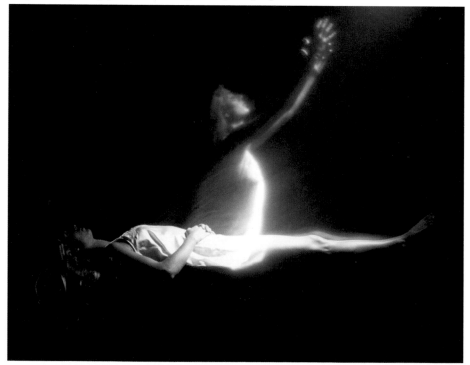

are outside our body but actually we are not. In other words, neuroscientists think OOBE is merely a hallucination.

Because science has no knowledge of the astral body, its characteristics or powers, it creates a model based merely on physiological and neurological evidence.

Contradictions

But certain facts contradict this. If OOBE is merely hallucination or a neural defect, how come there are people who see the astral body or etheric [not solid] double of someone having an OOBE? Sometimes the astral body is seen very far from the physical body of the sleeping person. If a theory contradicts a proven fact or experience, something's wrong with the theory.

Some scientists propose the most incredible theories just to maintain their own assumptions about the nature of physical reality. For example, one scientific theory on why natives of Fiji, Indonesia, Brazil, India and the Philippines are able to walk on fire is: "The natives have developed very powerful sweat glands on their feet, so that when they touch the burning charcoal or fire they are activated, thus cushioning the effects of the fire. The sweat glands cool the fire and therefore enable them to walk easily on it."

It would be nice if proponents of this theory tried walking barefooted on fire to test their theory.

Despite its obvious inadequacy (I walked on fire without getting hurt, although I don't have thick sweat glands), the theory is accepted by most scientists.

Near-Death Experience

Another phenomenon whose scientific explanation does not jibe with facts is near-death experience (NDE). In a typical NDE, as studied by Dr. Raymond Moody, a person is pronounced clinically dead. In

Descriptions of Near-Death Experiences

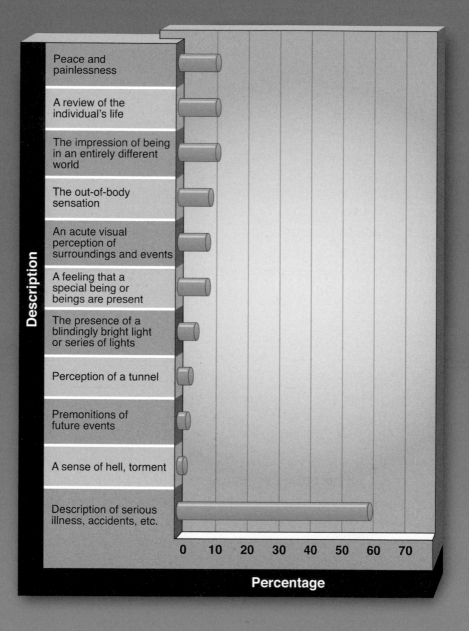

Description

- Peace and painlessness
- A review of the individual's life
- The impression of being in an entirely different world
- The out-of-body sensation
- An acute visual perception of surroundings and events
- A feeling that a special being or beings are present
- The presence of a blindingly bright light or series of lights
- Perception of a tunnel
- Premonitions of future events
- A sense of hell, torment
- Description of serious illness, accidents, etc.

0 10 20 30 40 50 60 70

Percentage

Taken from: George Gallup, Jr. and William Proctor, *Adventures in Immortality*, McGraw-Hill, 1982, pp. 200–201.

that state, the person sees himself traveling through a tunnel with a bright light at the end. He moves toward the light, usually seen as a being who asks him questions.

The being of light tells him it's not yet his time and to go back to earth. He wakes up feeling the pain of an accident if it is an accident or labor pains, etc. Then his/her life is transformed. He feels a sense of mission and exhibits previously absent psychic powers.

Scientists working with experimental pilots in Canada have a different explanation. They think NDE is caused by a lack of oxygen in the brain.

When pilots are in a rotating machine, the centrifugal force temporarily deprives the brain of oxygen. Pilots lose consciousness and get a sensation of floating or being out of the body and going through a tunnel where a seemingly [sic] being of light tells them it is not yet their time and they have to go back. They wake up remembering every detail of the incident, like in a typical NDE.

But there's one big difference. Pilots who experience this do not develop a sense of mission, neither do they acquire a new insight into their life. They are not transformed like those with actual NDE and do not develop psychic powers. These facts are ignored by scientists.

EVALUATING THE AUTHOR'S ARGUMENTS:

In this viewpoint Jaime T. Licauco writes, "If a theory contradicts a proven fact or experience, something's wrong with the theory." What kinds of evidence does he provide to counterbalance the scientific theories he criticizes? Do these anecdotes successfully cast doubt on the validity of the scientific research?

Intuition Can Defy Scientific Explanation

Nan O'Brien, interviewed by Jennifer Haupt

"Intuition is a catch-all phrase for the voice deep within us that resonates when it hears truth."

In the following viewpoint Jennifer Haupt interviews Nan O'Brien about her work as an intuitive counselor. For O'Brien, intuition is a sense of knowing something in the absence of intellectual proof, as well as a means of connecting with others beyond the physicality of the world. O'Brien does not use intuition to make predictions, because free will can change the outcome. But she believes that her intuition comes from a higher power, and she serves as a channel for information that people can use to see the life lesson plan for their lives and enable them to make better choices. O'Brien believes that everyone has intuition and that this ability can be developed with training.

Haupt has been a contributor to such magazines as *O, The Oprah Magazine* and *Reader's Digest*. She writes about those who find faith beyond religion and use it to change their lives and the lives of others. O'Brien is an internationally acclaimed author and a radio host.

AS YOU READ, CONSIDER THE FOLLOWING QUESTIONS:
1. What is a life lesson plan, as described by O'Brien?
2. What spiritual law does the author say operates in the case of life lesson plans?
3. What conflict arises when one attempts to trust or act on intuition, according to O'Brien?

Nan O'Brien didn't always embrace her intuitive gift, but now she uses it to help families to find closure with deceased loved ones, to help police departments find missing persons, and to help millions of people get in touch with what they really know about themselves, their desires, and their lives. Millions of people tune into her nationally syndicated radio show, read her books and go to see her at events, as well as hire her for private sessions. Here's why:

Jennifer Haupt: *How do you define* intuition?

Nan O'Brien: Intuition is a catch-all phrase for the voice deep within us that resonates when it hears truth. It is the sense we have of "knowing" in the absence of intellectual or tangible proof to support what we feel we know. It also is the vehicle of connectivity with others that is beyond the physicality of the world. Have you ever been thinking of someone you haven't heard from in a while, only to have that person call you on the phone a few moments later? Intuition is the mechanism that will have created that ability to have connected; there is no such thing as coincidence.

JH: *When people ask you questions on your radio show, are you using purely your psychic powers to find the answer, or also intuition?*

NO: I do not consider myself to possess "psychic powers," because I am not a "psychic." I do not make predictions, as I believe that we all have free will and free choice to make decisions for ourselves in this physical world. Therefore, predictions—more often than not— do not come true. For example, if a psychic predicts you will meet a man from Florida in six months, but in six months that man does not leave his home in Florida to move to where you are living, you will not meet him. If you have a soul contract with that man that is not realized, other spiritual laws will come into play, but no external power overrides our ability to choose for ourselves.

Now that I've said what I'm not, I'll explain what I am—an Intuitive Counselor. In answer to your question specifically, yes, I do use my intuition to respond to my callers or clients to counsel people, the same way that other professional counselors use psychology or therapeutic tools. In my belief system, the intuition, or "knowing-ness," comes from a Higher Power (I call it "God" but the name is unimportant), and the information comes through me, not from me. I am not allowed to censor, interpret, or "cherry pick" what I get. My function is only to act as the conduit, to pass along the information exactly as it is given to me.

My understanding is that we all have purpose in this existence, or a "life lesson plan," but we don't always remember why we came or what we wanted to learn. The life lesson plan juxtapositions against those people, circumstances, and/or situations that have come into a person's life, facilitating the learning and growth that person set out to accomplish.

It can be very powerful for a person to shift his or her thinking from "why me?" (not poor me) to "why did I attract this into my life? What do I need to learn? How can I grow from this situation?" It empowers a person to see his or her world through a prism of understanding purpose, and it can explain what has happened up till that point in a person's life, too, which can free one from feeling unlucky, or powerless in this world to do anything but react. It is spiritual law that once you learn a lesson it's yours—just as in school, once you take a test and pass, you do not have to take the test again—so it is also incredibly uplifting and empowering to know that what is behind you does not have to dictate what is in front of you, IF you learn the lesson.

Let's go back to the woman in the "Florida man" scenario. If the caller or client asked me whether they would be in a relationship in the future, I would start by looking at the reasons that person had not been in a healthy relationship up until that point. Did she have balance issues in life, i.e., gravitating toward emotionally unavailable men because she was more comfortable giving than receiving? Did she have trust or boundaries issues as a life lesson, which caused her to attract men in her life she needed to say no to? Being in a healthy relationship with self is a prerequisite to having a healthy relationship with someone else, but if we do not understand the why of how things have unfolded, we cannot change our choices.

"To listen to your instincts, press one."

"To listen to your instincts, press one," cartoon by Mike Baldwin, www.cartoonStock.com. Copyright © Mike Baldwin. Reproduction rights obtanable from www.CartoonStock.com.

JH: *Do you find that people are afraid of intuition? If so, why?*

NO: Afraid of intuition? Not necessarily. Afraid of my being intuitive? Sometimes. Especially men, who mistakenly think I can read their minds! Kidding aside, I don't know that people are afraid of their intuition so much as they are afraid to trust it. We all have intuition to some degree—it's like singing, we can all do it, but some should only sing in the shower!—but when we trust and act on our intuition and the outcome confirms its existence, it can be overwhelming and almost scary or "weird" for someone who is inclined to function in the "real" world.

The validation of trusting the intuition creates a clash between logic and experience. The logic says "rely on the five senses," while the experience says, "explain what just happened any other way than intuition." Over time, continually trusting our intuition lessens our conflict and moves us to "acceptance," which, by nature, is not fear-based, but faith-based.

JH: *Was there ever a time when you didn't trust your own intuition? How have you learned to trust it more over the years?*

NO: Absolutely! More times than I can count or care to remember, especially in my younger years. (smile) But, it soon became apparent that when I trusted my intuition, the outcomes were positive and when I didn't, the outcomes were "less positive"—they were the decisions I tended to regret. Like Pavlov, the successful use of the intuition conditioned me to be willing to trust it more, until I got to the point where I trusted my intuition implicitly.

Honestly, I could not do my radio, live event, or private sessions if I did not fully trust the process of intuitively "plugging in," allowing information to come through me, not from me. The trust in the intuition removes the ego from the process of Intuitive Counseling, and that is critical to its integrity, to the power of its truth. It's not about my being right or wrong in my responses, only that I give it to others as the information is given to me.

JH: *Can you teach people how to tap into their intuition?*

NO: Short answer: Yes. Long answer: While the experience of using one's intuition is a personal journey, there are exercises that can foster the ease with which you access it. Like any "exercise program," you get stronger through the repetition and consistent application of the exercises. By embracing the daily opportunities to practice using your intuition, you strengthen your willingness to then rely and act on it, perpetuating the four steps of faithful living: Acknowledgment, Trust, Reliance, Action.

The opportunities can be simple and a part of your life now, they don't have to be additions to your daily schedule. For example, if you work in a building with an elevator bank, stand in front of the elevator you intuitively feel is going to open (without cheating by listening or watching to see which direction an elevator is going). You will be amazed how often you are right—and that simple, daily affirmation feeds your willingness and ability to connect with your intuition in other ways—to call a friend who has been on your mind that, as it turns out, needed to hear from you; to drive a different route and find yourself helping a stranded elderly person on the side of a road you would not normally have traveled. It's not necessary to go climb a mountain to find yourself and your power.

EVALUATING THE AUTHOR'S ARGUMENTS:

Nan O'Brien, interviewed in this viewpoint by Jennifer Haupt, considers the source of intuition to be outside the individual. Compare this with the position of Carlin Flora, the author of the following viewpoint, who argues that intuition is a process performed within the individual by the unconscious mind. Which viewpoint do you favor? Explain your answer with evidence from each viewpoint.

Viewpoint 6

Intuition Has an Unconscious Cognitive Basis

Carlin Flora

"Think of [intuition] as rapid cognition or condensed reasoning that takes advantage of the brain's built-in shortcuts."

In the following viewpoint Carlin Flora describes intuition as an unconscious associative process or a mental matching game, in which the brain matches information from the senses against what it has stored within itself in order to make sense of the new information. Old information is stored as a mixture of fact and feeling, so when the brain matches a new situation to old information, it sends feelings and other sensory data to various parts of the body, especially the gut, along with the factual information. Flora suggests that the best approach to intuition is to study how the internalized experiences that give rise to intuitions can work with the conscious mind.

Flora is the author of numerous articles for *Psychology Today*.

AS YOU READ, CONSIDER THE FOLLOWING QUESTIONS:

1. According to Flora, how does cognitive scientist Alexandre Linhares think intuition can be described?
2. As reported by the author, in the study conducted by psychologist Antoine Bechara, what happened to brain-damaged patients who could not form emotional intuitions?
3. According to the author, how is intuition useful for answering trivia questions and tests?

Carlin Flora, "Gut Almighty," psychologytoday.com, May 1, 2007. Reproduced by permission.

I ntuition really does come from the gut. It's also a kind of matching game based on experience. There are times when trusting your gut is the smartest move—and times you'd better think twice.

You "know" things. You don't even know how you know them. Yet you have a sense of certainty when driving down a strange street that you really must make a left turn. Or comfort a co-worker who insists she's fine. Or quit your job and move to Paris.

Intuitions, or gut feelings, are sudden, strong judgments whose origin we can't immediately explain. Although they seem to emerge from an obscure inner force, they actually begin with a perception of something outside—a facial expression, a tone of voice, a visual inconsistency so fleeting you're not even aware you noticed.

Think of them as rapid cognition or condensed reasoning that takes advantage of the brain's built-in shortcuts. Or think of intuition as an unconscious associative process. Long dismissed as magical or beneath the dignity of science, intuition turns out to muster some fancy and fast mental operations. The best explanation psychologists now offer is that intuition is a mental matching game. The brain takes in a situation, does a very quick search of its files, and then finds its best analogue among the stored sprawl of memories and knowledge. Based on that analogy, you ascribe meaning to the situation in front of you. A doctor might simply glance at a pallid young woman complaining of fatigue and shortness of breath and immediately intuit she suffers from anemia.

The gut itself literally feeds gut feelings; think of butterflies in the stomach when a decision is pending. The gut has millions of nerve cells and, through them, a "mind of its own," says Michael Gershon, author of *The Second Brain* and a professor at Columbia University. Still, gut feelings do not originate there, but in signals from the brain.

That visceral punch in the paunch is testament that emotions are an intrinsic part of all gut feelings. "I don't think that emotion and intuition can be separated," says cognitive scientist Alexandre Linhares at the Brazilian School of Business and Public Administration. Emotion guides how we learn from experience; if you witness something while your adrenaline is pumping, for instance, it will be remembered very vividly.

Experience is encoded in our brains as a web of fact and feeling. When a new experience calls up a similar pattern, it doesn't unleash just stored knowledge but also an emotional state of mind and a predisposition to respond in a certain way. Imagine meeting a date who reminds you of loved ones and also of the emotions you've felt toward those people. Suddenly you begin to fall for him or her. "Intuition," says Linhares, "can be described as 'almost immediate situation understanding' as opposed to 'immediate knowledge.' Understanding is filled with emotion. We don't obtain knowledge of love, danger, or joy; we feel them in a meaningful way."

Encased in certainty, intuitions compel us to act in specific ways, and those who lack intuition are essentially cognitively paralyzed. Psychologist Antoine Bechara at the University of Southern California studied brain-damaged patients who could not form emotional intuitions when making a decision. They were left to decide purely via deliberate reasoning. "They ended up doing such a complicated analysis, factoring everything in, that it could take them hours to decide between two kinds of cereal," he says.

While endless reasoning in the absence of guiding intuitions is unproductive, some people, including [former] President [George W.] Bush, champion the other extreme—"going with the gut" at all times. Intuition, however, is best used as the first step in solving a problem or deciding what to do. The more experience you have in a particular domain, the more reliable your intuitions, because they arise out of the richest array of collected patterns of experience. But even in your area of expertise, it's wisest to test out your hunches—you could easily have latched on to the wrong detail and pulled up the wrong web of associations in your brain.

When researcher Douglas Hofstadter is starting a knotty math problem, for instance, he begins with a hunch. Then he hunkers down and calculates. After two weeks, perhaps he'll see a roadblock and give up. Another hunch pushes him to a new tack, and perhaps it is the right one.

It's time to declare an end to the battle between gut and mind—and to the belief that intuitions are parapsychological fluff. Better to explore how the internalized experiences from which gut feelings arise best interact with the deliberate calculations of the conscious mind.

Going with Your Gut Can Be a Winning Strategy for Trivia Games and Tests

You've memorized the almanac and you're ready to take down your Trivial Pursuit opponents. Well, don't get too cocky—sometimes

Psychologist Carl Jung (pictured) described intuition as the perception of realities that are unknown to the conscious mind. He said that intuition, sensing, feeling, and thinking are the four basic functions or ways of dealing with the world.

knowing less about a question helps you pick the correct answer. Intuition does the guesswork. Case in point: A kid is asked whether Spain or Portugal has a bigger population. He guesses Spain, simply because he's never even heard of Portugal. And he is right; there is a reason he isn't yet aware of Spain's less powerful and less populous neighbor. There is wisdom in his lack of knowledge, says Gerd Gigerenzer of the Max Planck Institute for Human Development in Berlin and author of *Gut Feelings.*

A University of London team found that people who went with their initial response on a test of visual perception (questions included picking out an anomaly in a pattern of symbols) did better than those who were given more time to ponder. Whereas the subconscious brain recognized a rotated version of the same symbol as different, the conscious brain reasoned that "an apple is still an apple whether rotated or not," the researchers concluded. When the subjects had time to engage their higher-level functions instead of relying on their intuitive responses, they were more likely to be wrong.

Jody Steinglass, founder of Empire Education, a private New York City–based tutoring company, says that the trick to preparing for standardized tests such as the [SAT I: Reasoning Test, a college entrance test] is to hone intuition by identifying cues—say, certain words—that let you know which category a question belongs to (quadratic equation), which in turn tells you how to solve it. "Right before test time, we go through drills where I will give students a list of questions. I don't have them actually solve them but just quickly tell me how they would solve each one. This way they are trained to make good snap judgments and then to confidently trust those judgments."

Big Purchases Benefit from Intuition, but Not Stock Picks

Our brains have a number of innate capacities, but they grow out of ancestral, not modern, problems, says Terry Burnham, author of *Mean Markets and Lizard Brains.* The types of dilemmas we are good at solving intuitively are ones in which the old machinery lines up well to produce positive contemporary outcomes. Investing is not among these.

Any gut feeling you may have about where to put your money is probably very similar to many others' gut feelings (say, going with a stock that has been on the upswing for a while). It's simply not investment-savvy to pick the same stocks as everyone else—you will not stand to gain.

Burnham advises that you set up a system to ensure that your prefrontal cortex, and not your gut, is firmly in charge of financial decisions. You need to analyze investment strategies and information about different companies. Just as Burnham refuses to get the key to the mini bar in hotel rooms lest he give in to a late-night junk-food craving, he "locks in" his money by making sure he can't change his allocations without an adviser's authorization. That way, he won't move his money around on a whim.

Intuition, however, is a reliable source of purchasing decisions, at least for big-ticket items. The only goal of investing money is to make a profit; cold calculations count. Material possessions, on the other hand, have a subjective value—you want products to bring some ease, comfort, or happiness.

When it comes to complex acquisitions such as homes and cars, consumer satisfaction is greater among buyers who decide with their gut. The experience of living in a house is ultimately an emotional and unpredictable one; so throw away your spreadsheet and rely on your "old brain" to assess whether or not you'll get more pleasure than pain out of the purchase. Resume rational deliberation for the little stuff; research shows it is superior to intuition for picking items such as oven mitts and shampoo.

It's comforting to know you can lean on your unconscious when facing big life questions. And, even better, you've got a mind that can both listen to the gut and keep it in line.

EVALUATING THE AUTHOR'S ARGUMENTS:

In this viewpoint Carlin Flora argues that intuition is a matching game carried out by the unconscious mind. Flora presents a number of situations that appear to involve intuition. How well does each of these fit the "matching game" definition? Explain, using evidence from the viewpoint.

Paranormal Research Is Legitimate Academic Study

Scott Carlson

"[The scholarly community is] not the haven of intellectual freedom that it is often cracked up to be."

In the following viewpoint reporter Scott Carlson features Stephen Braude, a professor of philosophy at the University of Maryland–Baltimore County. Although Braude had had a personal interest in the paranormal for years, he waited to stake his reputation on paranormal research until after he had already achieved respect in his field. He points to a long history of philosophical investigation of paranormal phenomena as the basis for his approach. Braude speaks to Carlson about the foundations of his research as well as about the unexpected resistance he has encountered from other members of the scholarly community.

Carlson is a senior reporter for *The Chronicle of Higher Education*. He often writes about architecture, sustainability, and environmental issues.

   1. According to Carlson, what graduate school experience first prompted Stephen Braude's interest in the paranormal?
   2. How does the author define "psychokinesis"?
   3. What academic milestone does the author say that Braude passed before he turned his research focus to the paranormal?

T he pivotal moment of Stephen E. Braude's academic career happened when he was in graduate school, on a dull afternoon in Northampton, Mass., in 1969.

Or, at least, what follows is what he says happened. Readers—skeptics and believers both—will have to make up their own minds.

Braude and two friends had seen the only movie in town and were looking for something to do. His friends suggested going to Braude's house and playing a game called "table up." In other words, they wanted to perform a seance.

They sat at a folding table, with their fingers lightly touching the tabletop, silently urging it to levitate. Suddenly it shuddered and rose several inches off the ground, then came back down. Then it rose a second time. And again and again. Braude and his friends worked out a code with the table, and it answered questions and spelled out names.

Braude says he had not given much thought to the paranormal before that afternoon, but the experience shook him to his core, he says, sitting in an easy chair in his immaculate home in suburban Baltimore. He insists there was no way his friends could have manipulated the table, adding, "I should tell you, we were not stoned."

An Academic Approach

Today Braude, 62, is one of the few mainstream academics applying his intellectual training to questions that many would regard at best as impossible to answer, and at worst absolutely ridiculous: Do psychic phenomena exist? Are mediums and ghosts real? Can people move objects with their minds or predict the future? A professor of philosophy at the University of Maryland–Baltimore County [UMBC], Braude is a past president of the Parapsychological Association, an organization that gathers academics and others interested in phenomena like

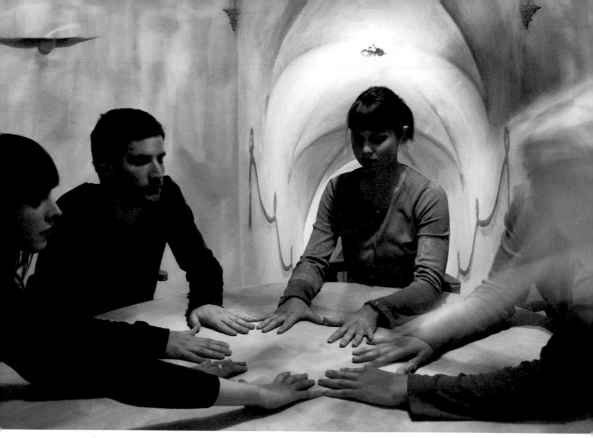

Stephen Braude, a philosophy professor at the University of Maryland–Baltimore County, says that he was first drawn to parapsychology after witnessing physical disturbances during a séance like the one pictured here.

ESP [extrasensory perception] and psychokinesis, and he has published a series of books with well-known academic presses on such topics.

His latest, *The Gold Leaf Lady and Other Parapsychological Investigations* (University of Chicago Press), is sort of a summing up of his career, filled with stories of people who claimed to have otherworldly abilities. The writing is so fluid that the book at times seems made for a screen adaptation. (In fact, Chris Carter, creator of *The X-Files*, contributes a blurb to the back of the book. Braude advised Carter on a screenplay he is writing.) But Braude also includes some dense philosophical arguments—especially in a chapter about synchronicity, in which he ponders whether humans can orchestrate unlikely coincidences through psychokinesis, the ability to move or influence objects with the mind.

"He is setting the standard for how an analytic philosopher who takes this stuff seriously should proceed," says Raymond Martin, chairman of the philosophy department at Union College, in New York, who formerly worked at the University of Maryland at College Park and met Braude then. "He's very thorough in informing himself about what has been shown empirically, and he is cautious. He is usually skeptical in the end, but he is not dismissive."

Martin thinks philosophers are often too quick to dismiss anything that smacks of exotic phenomena because they want to protect the integrity of the discipline. "A lot of people just don't want this stuff on the table, because they regard it as an embarrassment to philosophy," he says. "Steve does take it seriously, and he has paid a price."

Thought Experiments

Greg Ealick took several of Braude's classes 20 years ago when he was an undergraduate at UMBC, and he is now Braude's colleague as an adjunct instructor in the philosophy department there. He says the philosophical aspects of Braude's work are "first-rate," although he's not convinced of the science of researching paranormal phenomena.

Braude's explorations could be seen as thought experiments, he says. Common in philosophy, such experiments pose odd scenarios to test arguments. A particularly well-known one asks: What if your brain were pulled out of your skull, put into a vat, and hooked up to a computer that could keep it alive and simulate external stimuli? Would you know that you were no longer inside your body? Therefore, can you know anything about the external world? "A lot of first-rate philosophy of mind comes from wildly speculative thought experiments," Ealick says. "I don't think that Steve's are really any wilder than the rest."

After his experience with the table in Northampton, Braude says, he put the event out of his mind for almost a decade. He got a job at the University of Maryland in 1971, and he went about publishing

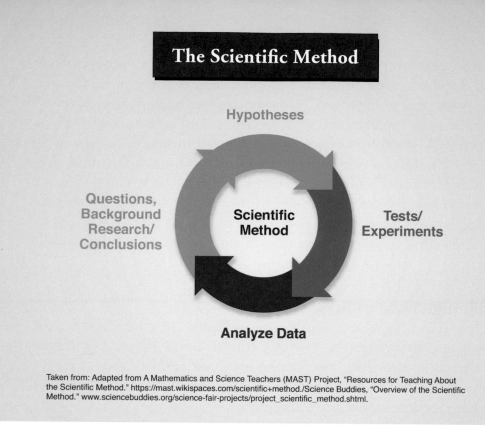

The Scientific Method

Hypotheses

Questions, Background Research/ Conclusions

Scientific Method

Tests/ Experiments

Analyze Data

Taken from: Adapted from A Mathematics and Science Teachers (MAST) Project, "Resources for Teaching About the Scientific Method." https://mast.wikispaces.com/scientific+method./Science Buddies, "Overview of the Scientific Method." www.sciencebuddies.org/science-fair-projects/project_scientific_method.shtml.

articles on the philosophy of time and the philosophy of language for the next seven years, until he got tenure.

Jaded Perspective

Then he came out, so to speak. He knew that philosophers, like William James and later H.H. Price, had studied paranormal phenomena such as spiritualism and life after death. He thought he could demonstrate to colleagues that such phenomena were still worth studying. "To show you how naive I was, I actually thought that they would be pleased to discover that they were wrong, so long as that brought them closer to discovering the truth." Instead, many shunned him.

"It clarified for me a lot about the scholarly community generally, something that has been confirmed over and over and over," he says. "It's not the haven of intellectual freedom that it is often cracked up to be."

Some of that jaded perspective comes through in *The Gold Leaf Lady*, which Braude describes as his "kiss-and-tell book" about his paranormal research. He trashes plenty of people in the book, including supposed psychics and their handlers who appear to be frauds. But he saves his sharpest barbs for prominent skeptics, like Paul Kurtz, a professor emeritus of philosophy at the State University of New York at Buffalo and founder of the Committee for Skeptical Inquiry, and James Randi, a magician better known as the Amazing Randi. Randi is described as a "publicity hound" who "weaseled out" of a challenge to explain phenomena produced by Ted Serios, who some believe could make odd and spooky images appear on Polaroid film. Kurtz is described as "disreputable" and sloppy. The skeptics, Braude says, pick out the weakest cases and demolish them, then use those spectacular debunkings to persuade the public that all exotic claims are bosh.

EVALUATING THE AUTHOR'S ARGUMENTS:

At the end of this viewpoint by Scott Carlson, Stephen Braude suggests that prominent skeptics often point to the weakest arguments for paranormal phenomena to discredit all evidence. In viewpoints like the following one by Robert Klose, which is written from a skeptical point of view, do you see evidence of tactics like those Braude discusses?

"The paranormal offers all that the grind of scientific research does not: immediate gratification, pat explanations, and the reduction of complex matters to fleeting sounds and images."

Paranormal and Pseudoscience Detract from Legitimate Science

Robert Klose

Robert Klose is a professor who has been teaching biology to college students for a number of years. In this viewpoint he argues that student interest and belief in the paranormal not only disrupts his classroom environment but actively impedes students' ability to grasp scientific principles. Because students have grown used to the easy answers provided by paranormal phenomena, they are unwilling or unable to do the hard work of grasping scientific concepts and engaging in scientific research. Klose challenges teachers to confront this mindset head on, to convince students of the essential importance of science to society.

Klose is an associate professor of biological science at the University of Maine at Augusta. He is a frequent contributor to *The Christian Science Monitor* and the author of the book *Small Worlds: Adopted Sons, Pet Piranhas, and Other Mortal Concerns.*

Robert Klose, "Atoms vs. a Three-Legged Woman?," *Phi Delta Kappan,* vol. 90, no. 10, June 2009, pp. 767–769.

AS YOU READ, CONSIDER THE FOLLOWING QUESTIONS:
1. What subject was Klose teaching in the anecdote that opens this viewpoint?
2. Which concepts are harder to grasp, according to the author— scientific principles or paranormal phenomena?
3. Whom does Klose quote near the end of the viewpoint as inspiration for teachers who want to overcome their students' resistance to hard science?

In my college course in introductory biology, I include a few lectures on the structure of the atom as a basis for understanding the chemistry of living things. To convey how incredibly small these particles are, I point out that Danish physicist Niels Bohr described the modern atomic model in 1913, but that we couldn't actually see an atom until the 1980s when IBM researchers photographed atoms using a Scanning Tunneling Microscope. Soon after—as a sort of encore—this instrument was used to manipulate 35 atoms of the gas xenon—and later, the very heavy metal thorium—into a pattern, a corporate logo to be exact. And which logo would that be?

Why, IBM, of course.

When I tell my students about this, many—but not all—of them are duly wowed. But once, a student spoke up and decreed that atoms didn't exist. His reasoning: If they were so elusive and virtually invisible, how could they constitute substances as dense as metals? Furthermore, he asked how such exceedingly small things—mere will o' the quantum wisps—could be shuffled around, even by IBM.

Skepticism Is Necessary

Let me begin by reaffirming, in writing, my belief that skepticism is necessary in any discipline, but especially in science, where experimental findings must rest on a veritable Masada of data in order to be taken seriously by the scientific community. Every scientist worth his or her salt has a duty to listen to new information with an attentive but always critical ear. For every nod of the head as one considers new data, there should be four or five impatient taps of the pencil on the desktop (I think this is the correct ratio). The result is a set of results that emerges from the crucible of cross-examination, ready for general dissemination.

Like most teachers I know, I encourage critical thinking in my classes. "Dissect the knowledge, don't worship it," I tell my students. Challenge me. Ask questions. Hold me to account for what I teach. (Neils Bohr used to tell his students, "Every sentence that I utter should be regarded by you not as an assertion but as a question.") This is, more or less, what my student, that atom-doubter, did, and though it would have been nice if he hadn't ruled out the existence of atoms with such finality. How could I object to his putting my intellectual feet to the fire and compelling me to explain the concept further, to the point where understanding was a real possibility?

Scientific Information Is Easily Rejected

However, I was troubled by his tendency—shared by other of my students over the years—to reject scientific information out of hand. Atoms, genetics, plate tectonics, evolution (especially evolution!)—all have fallen victim to their terrible swift sword not of doubt, but of outright disbelief. They are not usually hostile to the information; they simply convey the impression that I must be, somehow, mistaken.

This I can live with. What bamboozles me is that students who sniff at DNA's role in determining our physical and, to an extent, behavioral characteristics frequently embrace paranormal and even atrocious "*Enquirer*-caliber" claims whole hog. Secret human/animal hybrid experiments, crop circles, Martian civilizations, invisible atmospheric jellyfish creatures, and jackalopes make their way down my students' mental gullets without a hitch. If they're willing to accept such unsubstantiated things at face value, why can't they be receptive to knowledge acquired via the scientific method? How can a student doubt that the continents are adrift, yet seize the idea of alien abductions with such dire passion?

This very thought was brought home to me years ago when I was walking the minefield of evolution in my general biology course. As I described the evolution of the modern horse from small, puppy dog–size ancestors, a student named Brian expressed his skepticism, using the words "You've got to be kidding" for emphasis. When I asked if anyone could describe the evolution of another species, Brian volunteered that "I once saw a three-legged woman in a porno magazine. It was amazing. I said to myself, is this evolution?"

At first, I thought he was joking, so I smiled benignly and stared into the distance. But his comment had electrified the class (late on a Friday afternoon, when they were normally as torpid as clams at low tide). They became intensely interested in this unfortunate woman, and fell into animated chatter, wanting to know where they could get the magazine with the corroborating image.

I eventually brought the class under control, though they grew resentful when I discounted Brian's story. The thing was, he had been absolutely serious (I can still see his face, earnest and open, seeking only my approval). In fact, if our classroom had been a ship, the crew of students, given a choice between my navigational course and the one Brian had set, would have strung me up from the yardarm and awarded him sash and sword.

According to the author, some students today seem more accepting of subjects such as crop circles (pictured), human-animal hybrid experiments, and Martian civilizations than they are in accepting the role of DNA as the determiner of our physical and behavioral characteristics.

Real Science Versus Paranormal

Evolution isn't the only thing that brings out false as well as fabulous associations in students' minds. The same occurs with other areas of science, especially if they're theoretical or cutting edge: Real-world scientific goings-on incur student doubt, while their faith in the fringe and paranormal aspects of science remains boundless. Thus, when I address conditions that promote human twinning, students assail me with questions about Siamese twins conjoined at the genitalia; when I describe the mechanics of cloning simple cells, they profess that the government has been secretly cloning human automatons for years; when I outline mechanisms of genetic mutation, students envision someone sprouting a second head.

In Brian's very same class, when I announced that we would be studying chemistry for two weeks as preamble to the biological topics to follow, a student immediately asked: "Are we going to blow things up?"

US Public's Beliefs in Evolution

On December 17, 2010, a Gallup Poll asked members of the public to declare which of the statements below most closely approximated their views on the origin and development of human beings.

Belief System:	Creationist View	Theistic Evolution	Naturalistic Evolution
Beliefs	God created man pretty much in his present form at one time within the last 10,000 years.	Man has developed over millions of years from less advanced forms of life, but God guided this process, including man's creation.	Man has developed over millions of years from less advanced forms of life. God had no part in this process.
Everyone	**40%**	**38%**	**16%**
Postgraduate	22%	49%	25%
College graduate	37%	38%	21%
Some college	44%	36%	16%
High school diploma or less	47%	34%	9%

Taken from: Gallup Poll, December 17, 2010. www.gallup.com/poll/145286/four-americans-believe-strict-creationism.aspx.

Science seldom involves "blowing things up." Many scientific ideas are explosive in their implications, but the research leading to a data-based conclusion involves a lot of tedium (i.e., somebody has got to wash test tubes and crunch numbers). To achieve a reasonable grasp of a scientific concept, some depth of understanding—education—is in order. Thus, the idea of the sheer diversity of life on Earth is startling, but a discussion of the mechanisms and conditions which made that life possible in the first place involves an understanding of atomic bonding, thermodynamics, and gas exchange across the cell membrane. Most of these processes can't be seen in any direct way: Oxygen and carbon dioxide are invisible; microscopes aren't yet powerful enough to resolve atomic structure; and heat can only be felt (and imaged in the abstract). However, these processes are measurable, but measurement involves numbers and instrumentation and time and . . . well, you get the picture. Science is hard.

> ## FAST FACT
>
> In a 2009 Harris Interactive poll, 45 percent of surveyed American adults said they believe in Darwin's theory of evolution; the same poll showed that 42 percent of people believe in ghosts and 32 percent believe in UFOs.

In contrast to mainstream science, paranormal phenomena do have the effect of "blowing things up" because they offer big, grand, gorgeous images that even the uninitiated can grasp and thrill to at first blush. It makes little difference if one has never seen Bigfoot, an alien, or a human clone. There are those who claim they have, and many, many others are eager to vouch for their existence by proxy.

Fleeting Satisfaction

The paranormal, in short, promises absolute answers in the here and now. It belongs to popular, not scientific, culture. As such, the paranormal offers all that the grind of scientific research does not: immediate gratification, pat explanations, and the reduction of complex matters to fleeting sounds and images. This expectation of ready answers is poor preparation for a scientific vocation, where the measured steps of laboratory research are often less than thrilling and their denouement [result] seldom gripping.

But to precipitate an extraterrestrial as a substitute for an understanding of the physics underlying astronomy—now, that's science as popular culture likes it: low calorie, low carb, yet sweet.

The only problem is that popular culture, while seductive and fleetingly satisfying, is not transmissible. Check that. What I mean is that there is no value in transmitting it. Consider: What father would sit his five-year-old son upon his knee and begin, "Now, Ernest, let's talk about UFOs so that, some day, you can tell your children what we know about the universe." But the transmission of real science improves us as a species. Lacking instinct as we do, science is the only option for the constructive development of modern society, which has become, for better and sometimes worse, a technocracy [a society governed by those who have mastered technology].

A Stumbling Block

The upshot of all this is that the far greater allure of the paranormal and pseudoscientific has impeded students' ability to grapple with the concepts and precepts of so-called "hard science." Such grappling brings them only frustration and desperation when they're confronted with ideas that 1) demand that they think, 2) are perceived as irrelevant to their experience, and 3) like Darwin's theory of natural selection, depend to some extent on inference and deductive reasoning. Thus, they're unwilling to believe that humans descended from a lower order of animals, but they're already sold on our species' evolutionary future. They envision throbbing buttheads suspended in the universal ether, radiating lethal levels of I.Q. and communicating with telepathy. Embracing such a fantastic idea is much less stressful because it's intellectually trivial, requires no dreaded math, and offers the sense that one is dabbling in the scientific. Aficionados of this stuff can find no comfortable place to sit at the banquet of mainstream science, so they sate themselves with Mc-Science, emphasizing convenience and speed over diet.

This imp of the paranormal bites students with the tenacity of a deer tick and persists like Lyme disease; but students are weakened by this because it convinces them that knowledge is easy to come by. The teacher interested in turning back this tide of ignorance might consider [Albert] Einstein, who said, "As the size of a circle of light increases, so does the circumference of darkness around it." What he was alluding to, of course, was that the more we learn, the more questions we raise. (Mark Twain struck the same theme in a more jocose [humorous] way when he wrote, "Scientists have raised so many questions about the subject that we shall soon know nothing about it at all.") The challenge is to convey this to students without frustrating them, to portray science as an invitation rather than the labor of Sisyphus [a mythical figure whom the Greek gods required to repeatedly push a boulder up a hill]. The dedicated and creative teacher knows what to do.

Which leaves me with several questions: If UFOs have visited Earth, why do they always abduct a bumpkin sitting in a rowboat in the middle of Maine? Why don't they ever take a surgeon? Or a president? Why don't they ever take me?

EVALUATING THE AUTHOR'S ARGUMENTS:

In this viewpoint Robert Klose suggests that the popularity of the paranormal actively hurts his students' ability to grasp scientific concepts. Based on your experience in learning science and your observations of your classmates and teachers, do you agree or disagree with this argument? Explain your answer.

Chapter 2

Why Do People Believe in Paranormal Phenomena?

Some people think that belief in the paranormal is a normal brain function; others characterize the belief as a form of mental illness.

Belief in the Paranormal Has a Neuroscientific Basis

Clare Wilson

"The better you are at tuning in to your subconscious, the more likely you are to believe in the paranormal."

Although a large percentage of people believe in unexplained phenomena, believers are often dismissed by academics, journalists, and the educated public as being gullible or uneducated. In this viewpoint, however, Clare Wilson argues that believers in the paranormal may actually just be more tuned in to their surroundings, particularly to subconscious stimuli, than their nonbelieving peers are. Experiments have revealed that people who self-identify as believers in paranormal phenomena also score higher on tests designed to measure sensitivity to subconscious sensory input.

Wilson is the medical features editor for *New Scientist* magazine. She has also written for the UK medical magazine *Hospital Doctor* and the pharmaceutical newsletter *Scrip*. Wilson has a degree in cell biology from the University of Manchester.

AS YOU READ, CONSIDER THE FOLLOWING QUESTIONS:
1. What two animals does Wilson use as metaphors for people who believe in paranormal phenomena and those who do not?
2. According to the author, what are some tasks at which people who believe in the paranormal excel?
3. How does the author define the term "transliminality"?

It is five minutes past midnight and I am alone in my house. I am working late, and the only illumination is the blue-white glow from my laptop computer. I live in a quiet London suburb, and at this time of night distractions are confined to the occasional eerie screeches and hisses from marauding urban foxes.

I pick up the phone to call Michael Thalbourne, a psychologist at the University of Adelaide in Australia. I want to talk to him about his research on chance, coincidence and the paranormal. Although the interview time has not been prearranged, we have been in contact by email, so it is disconcerting to hear a long pause when I introduce myself. When Thalbourne eventually speaks he sounds taken aback. "I was right in the middle of typing out an email to you," he says.

Thalbourne's instinct is to suspect some paranormal explanation for our synchronicity [events that occur simultaneously for no apparent reason]. My gut reaction is to suggest a more mundane alternative. It looks as if he is what some psychologists would call a sheep, while I am a goat.

The animal terminology stems from a passage in the Bible about a shepherd sorting through his flock to separate the sheep—representing the nations that believe in God—from the goats, or those that do not. Thalbourne and his ilk, however, are interested in belief in the paranormal and supernatural. And such beliefs turn out to be surprisingly common. For example, a 1998 survey of 1000 adults in the UK showed that one-third believed in fortune telling, half believed in telepathy, and a whopping two-thirds agreed with the statement that some people have powers that science cannot explain.

Decades of scientific research into parapsychology have produced no convincing demonstration of the paranormal that can be reliably reproduced—the acid test of scientific inquiry. So why should scientists be so interested in whether or not people believe in it? Research into the differences between sheep and goats has over the years produced some intriguing findings about how the brain works.

Sheep Versus Goats
Until recently, sheep might have been forgiven for being cheesed off by all this research—most of the findings were less than complimentary about them. Study after study suggested that sheep saw paranormal events where there were none, simply because they were worse at judging probabilities and randomness, and even at using logical reasoning. But newer research might restore some sheepish pride. It turns out that the kind of thinking involved in belief in the paranormal helps us carry out a range of important cognitive tasks, from spotting predators to recognising familiar faces. Sheep also tend to be more imaginative and more creative. Some psychologists even think that people who believe they have paranormal powers such as telepathy, dreams that foretell the future, or other forms of

A Londoner has his fortune told. A 1998 survey found that one-third of British people believed in fortune-telling, half believed in telepathy, and two-thirds thought people have powers that science cannot explain.

extrasensory perception (ESP) might actually be accessing information stored in their subconscious without realising it.

Imagine, for example, that you are walking along the street with your old friend Bob, when you start thinking about a mutual college chum, Joe. "I wonder what Joe Smith is getting up to these days," you say. "That's amazing!" says Bob. "I was just thinking of Joe myself." You believe it is simply a coincidence. Bob suspects some form of telepathy. But there is a third explanation: without being consciously aware of it, both you and Bob noticed something that reminded you of Joe. Maybe you passed someone who looked just a little bit like him, or maybe it was something in a shop window that reminded you of him.

Transliminality

It was Thalbourne who first suggested that people who regularly have subconscious information such as this surfacing in their conscious mind would often seem to require the paranormal to explain their experiences. He coined the term "transliminality" for this tendency for information to pass between our subconscious and our conscious mind. He has also designed a questionnaire to measure transliminality. It asks questions such as how good people are at using their imagination, whether they have a heightened awareness of sights and sound and whether they have ever felt they have received "special wisdom". Thalbourne and others have shown in several studies that transliminality corresponds to where people fall on a sheep-goat scale. In other words, the better you are at tuning in to your subconscious, the more likely you are to believe in the paranormal.

This correlation alone suggests Thalbourne may be onto something. And in 2002, a group at Goldsmiths College in London reported an intriguing practical demonstration of transliminality. They asked people to take part in an apparent test of ESP with Zener cards, which display one of five symbols: a circle, a cross, a square, a star or three

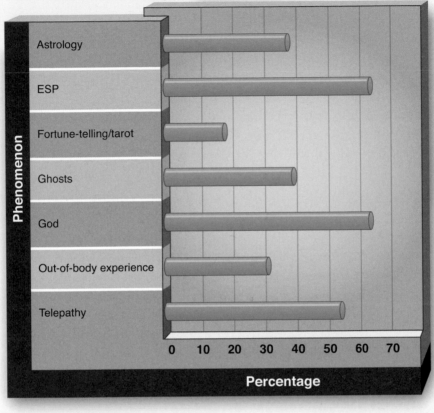

Percentage of UK Residents Who Believe in Various Phenomena, 1998

Phenomenon (top to bottom): Astrology, ESP, Fortune-telling/tarot, Ghosts, God, Out-of-body experience, Telepathy

Percentage (x-axis): 0 10 20 30 40 50 60 70

Taken from: Ipsos MORI, 1998.

wavy lines. The subjects sat in front of a computer monitor displaying the back of a card. They pressed a key to choose which symbol they thought it was. Then they got to see the card's face.

Subliminal Clues

What they did not know was that they were being given subliminal clues as to which symbol was about to appear. Before a card's back was shown, they saw a flash of its face lasting for just 14.3 milliseconds, too fast for most people to register. Some participants, however, were able to subconsciously pick up on the clue, and as a result they scored better than chance at predicting which symbol would appear. "To those participants it would appear that they had ESP abilities," says psychologist Chris French, who led the research. And people who were best at picking up the subliminal image also turned out to be the most transliminal as measured by Thalbourne's questionnaire. It was a neat demonstration of how access to subconscious information can give the appearance of psychic abilities. . . .

As a goat myself, I tend to opt for down-to-earth explanations. Here, for example, is how I account for the fact that Thalbourne was emailing me just as I phoned for that interview. Earlier that day, while it was already night-time in Adelaide, I had sent him an email asking if we could arrange a time to talk. Later I decided to chance a phone call anyway, and not wanting to stay up working any longer than necessary, I called at midnight my time, or 8.30 am in Adelaide, which I figured was probably the earliest he would arrive at his office. He had actually got to work shortly before, and started his day as many of us do by turning on his computer and was responding to the emails he received overnight—which happened to include one from me.

Thalbourne, however, persists in viewing the event as one of life's intriguing little coincidences. But then he does happily admit to being a sheep. "My life is full of many small and occasionally large coincidences that suggest some unusual form of cause and effect," he says. "I believe that I can't disbelieve in it."

EVALUATING THE AUTHOR'S ARGUMENTS:

Clare Wilson, who identifies herself as a nonbeliever in psychic phenomena, comes up with a down-to-earth explanation for the coincidence that opens the viewpoint. To what would you attribute this apparent episode of synchronicity?

Belief in the Paranormal May Be Linked to Mental Illness

"Depression, dissociation, and the hyperactive or impulsive component of ADHD . . . were associated with tendencies toward paranormal beliefs."

Matthew J. Sharps, Justin Matthews, and Janet Asten

In the following viewpoint Matthew J. Sharps, Justin Matthews, and Janet Asten argue that observations attributed to the paranormal come from a mistaken interpretation of known phenomena and are triggered by something that the individual perceives. They suggest that stress, arousal, and high levels of scene complexity and activity lead to a more imaginative reconstruction of events. In addition, they hypothesize—and their study finds—that people with attention-deficit/hyperactivity disorder, depression, and dissociation (a feeling of being removed from the everyday world) are more likely to be associated with certain types of paranormal beliefs.

At the time of writing, Sharps, Matthews, and Asten were working in the Department of Psychology at California State University–Fresno.

Matthew J. Sharps, Justin Matthews, and Janet Asten, "Cognition and Belief in Paranormal Phenomena: Gestalt/Feature-Intensive Processing Theory and Tendencies Toward ADHD, Depression, and Dissociation," *The Journal of Psychology*, vol. 140, November 2006. Copyright © 2006. Reproduced by permission of Taylor & Francis Group, LLC, www.taylorandfrancis.com and Matthew J. Sharps.

Most evidence suggests that paranormal observations result from erroneous interpretation of known phenomena. Most paranormal observations can probably be explained by psychology. Thus, it is important to understand the psychological dynamics underlying belief systems that may predispose individuals to make erroneous interpretations. In our research, we did not study the possible existence of cryptids or paranormal phenomena. Instead, we focused on the psychological dynamics underlying the relevant belief systems.

The bulk of erroneous observations of atypical phenomena are psychologically explicable, especially within the realms of psychology dealing with eyewitness identification. For example, UFO sightings do not typically result from eyewitness observations of a dark sky. There is usually a light, a cloud, or an oddly lit aircraft involved. The Loch Ness monster, when allegedly shown in photographs, rarely arises from a lack of visual stimuli on a calm lake; it frequently turns out to be a school of salmon or a flock of ducks. In the majority of cases, something initiates a person's perception of the monster. In Bigfoot sightings, which frequently occur in the dark or under other suboptimal viewing conditions, the disturbed brush and marks in the ground indicate that the observation is derived from the presence of something. The thing in question is more likely to have been a practical joker, a foraging bear, or an angry cow than an unknown hominid. . . .

Although a variety of situational and psychophysiological factors interact to reduce the accuracy of memory, [British psychologist Frederic C.] Bartlett was able to show that memories, in general, reconfigure in the directions of gist, brevity, and personal belief. Criticisms of Bartlett's work have now been largely reconciled with reference to methodological differences, and the trends identified by Bartlett have recently been replicated.

A recent theoretical formulation, gestalt/feature-intensive processing theory [G/FI] is instrumental in further conceptualizing the dynamics underlying these reconfigurations. According to G/FI theory, under stress or under suboptimal viewing conditions, the feature-intensive processing of the details of a memory or mental representation is diminished, yielding a gestalt representation of an event or of a given class of event that is relatively barren of details. Such details would help to anchor that memory to the physical reality it represents, but, because the details are reduced in number and significance, the resulting gestalt is more amenable to change or to the addition of erroneous details that may arise from postevent information or from characteristics or cognitive frameworks brought by the witness to the situation.

These reconfigurative tendencies are significantly exacerbated by stress and arousal, scene complexity, and surrounding activity. The dynamics underlying the effects of arousal (e.g., on identification accuracy) are still the subject of debate. However, literature on this subject suggests that factors such as stress, arousal, and high levels of scene complexity and activity result in a greater degree of imaginative reconstruction of events than is likely to occur in their absence. The nonexistent Japanese ships, aircraft, and fleets observed by American soldiers in Hawaii after the attack on Pearl Harbor are examples. In another example, U.S. Army survivors at Little Bighorn immediately after the annihilation of [General George Armstrong] Custer's command saw nonexistent cavalry rescue parties and interpreted Sioux and Cheyenne warriors as American cavalry in several instances. A third example is eyewitness reports of a Washington, DC, sniper's white or cream-colored van, when the vehicle was actually a dark blue Chevrolet Caprice.

FAST FACT

So-called flying saucer cults include the Heaven's Gate cult, which inspired thirty-nine people in California to commit suicide in March 1997.

In summary, when people are stressed or subject to complex, unfamiliar environments, they are likely to reconfigure objects, people, and events into other objects, people, and events, as shown by Bartlett and as further elaborated recently in G/FI theory. However, even under extreme circumstances, not all people perceive objects as other entities. Thus, factors inherent in individual differences must be involved. In the following paragraphs, we suggest possible factors that lead to differential perceptions.

Tendency to exhibit features of attention deficit hyperactivity disorder (ADHD), and especially tendency toward the hyperactive or impulsive pattern shown in specific manifestations of the disorder, may exacerbate tendency to exhibit the type of reconfiguration discussed in the previous paragraphs. The diagnosable syndrome does not need to be present for an individual to show such tendencies. ADHD symptoms tend to be continuously distributed in large populations (i.e., a person can have ADHD tendencies without having diagnosable ADHD, and recent researchers found that such tendencies at a subclinical level can significantly affect behaviors such as substance abuse.

Although the potential ramifications have been overblown in the popular media, specific aspects of ADHD, including hyperfocus, tendencies toward rapid task-shifting, and hyperactivity, would probably have been assets, rather than liabilities, in the ancient world of hunting and gathering. [M.J.] Sharps, [A.B.] Villegas, [S.S] Nunes, and [T.L.] Barber found that specific cognitive aspects of the hunting world are still present and experimentally accessible in modern humans. We suggest that in some individuals, adaptations that may have been advantageous when humans were hunter-gatherers are still present and are potentially disadvantageous today. These individuals might be more attracted to a world of unknown animals and unexplored possibilities, in part as a refuge from the modern world to which specific aspects of their intellects and psyches are unsuited. We hypothesized that such individuals may be predisposed to beliefs in cryptids because these could represent unknown forms of life. However, we did not expect subclinical ADHD tendencies to be associated with similar beliefs in ghosts, telepathy, or astrology. Because these paranormal beliefs are irrelevant to hunting and related evolutionary processes, we did not expect them to appeal to people with tendencies toward ADHD.

We did not expect to find the same pattern of beliefs in people with symptoms of depression. Unknown animals might not hold special appeal for people with depression, but we hypothesized that potential avenues of escape from perceived difficulties would. Depressed individuals might be more likely to believe in ghosts, for example, because ghosts provide evidence for an afterlife in which present stress would be eliminated. We expected that belief in UFOs would be another avenue of escape for depressed individuals. Thus, we hypothesized that individuals with subclinical tendencies toward depression would have elevated beliefs in the existence of UFOs and ghosts, but not in cryptids.

We hypothesized that a third psychological condition, dissociation, also influences paranormal beliefs. People in dissociative states feel separated in conscious awareness from ordinarily familiar information or emotional states. "Part of the person . . . is elsewhere and not available at the present time." Even at the subclinical levels addressed in the present article, people with dissociative tendencies feel somewhat removed from the everyday world of human experience. Individuals with dissociative tendencies exhibit diminished critical assessment of reality and may have paranormal beliefs at higher levels than do individuals in the general population. However, we did not expect these tendencies to be more prevalent in one area of paranormal phenomena than in others. . . .

Discussion

The results of this research supported our hypotheses: Depression, dissociation, and the hyperactive or impulsive component of ADHD, as measured in nondiagnosed adults by appropriate standardized instruments, were associated with tendencies toward paranormal beliefs. Also as predicted, different types of paranormal beliefs were associated with different psychological tendencies. Dissociation was associated with enhanced levels of paranormal beliefs overall, but not with any specific type of belief. This result may reflect gestalt tendencies—or tendencies toward the relatively rapid but general appraisal of stimuli, with limited attention to specific features or internal consistencies within those stimuli—that one would expect to find in individuals with dissociative tendencies, even at the subclinical level. Having

According to the author, individuals who suffer from such frustrating psychological conditions as ADHD, depression, and dissociation have a tendency to believe in the paranormal, suggesting that they reconstruct sensory input along lines that may lessen their mental stress.

depressive tendencies was associated with ghost-related ideation, the only belief about the afterlife we examined. Last, both depression and the hyperactive aspect of ADHD were associated with ADHD ideation (respectively, $p = .032$ and $p = .031$), and hyperactivity was significantly associated with cryptozoological beliefs ($p = .03$). However, when we substituted overall ADHD tendencies for the F scale of the CAARS [Conners Adult ADHD Rating Scales], this relationship was no longer significant. This result indicated that the hyperactive or impulsive component of ADHD behavior predisposes individuals to believe in creatures such as Bigfoot and aliens. The result is consistent with our hypothesis that this ADHD-cryptozoological belief relationship may be related to human adaptations to the requirements of a hunter-gather lifestyle.

Our findings suggest that individuals prone to paranormal and cryptozoological beliefs tend to have systematically identifiable patterns of psychological characteristics (i.e., tendency toward ADHD, depression, and dissociation). These patterns are observable even when the psychological tendencies are present at nondiagnosable (i.e., low) levels, such as in our nonclinical sample of university students.

It is important to note that we would not expect all individuals who express paranormal or cryptozoological beliefs or who are interested in these topics to have tendencies toward ADHD, depression, and dissociation. Individuals could arrive at these beliefs from a variety of directions and perspectives, ranging from familial or environmental influences that spurred the interests to personal experiences with phenomena that were perceived to be paranormal. There are many reasons that people may become interested in atypical phenomena. Despite this qualification, these psychological associations did exist in our sample, suggesting that people with these patterns of symptoms may interpret sensory information in paranormal or cryptozoological terms. These interpretive predispositions may then influence the way people remember and report the phenomena.

Such influences on memory and reporting are of critical significance. Memories are popularly seen as fixed, more similar to a veridical photograph than to a malleable representation. However, Bartlett found that memory is subject to significant reconfiguration. The interpretation and conclusions of any memory are subject to the effects of reconfigurations. Many researchers found that the information an individual has prior to an event has powerful biasing effects on memory and interpretation of that event, in realms as disparate as text processing, visual and verbal memory, and interpretation of forensically relevant stimuli and complex crime scenes. Thus, it is important to understand the predisposing influences that act upon the belief structures that may predispose an individual to perceive a UFO rather than a cloud, or a Bigfoot rather than a bear running at twilight. These perceptions, transformed by the overall constellation of predisposing influences, become the reconfigured memories that are then interpreted and reinterpreted by the given individual.

We found that systematic, predictable constellations of psychological characteristics accompany predisposing belief systems in a peripheral area of human psychology, the study of the paranormal and the cryptozoological beliefs. Future researchers should look for similar patterns in the less marginal areas of eyewitness identification in crime and the report of significant events in clinical, counseling, and educational applications.

EVALUATING THE AUTHOR'S ARGUMENTS:

In this viewpoint Matthew J. Sharps, Justin Matthews, and Janet Asten argue that certain disorders or mental illness are likely to be associated with certain paranormal beliefs. They also suggest that people prone to paranormal beliefs tend to exhibit these psychological characteristics. What is the difference between these two statements? For which of them do you think the authors provided the most evidence? Explain your answer using evidence from the viewpoint.

Belief in the Paranormal Is a Normal Brain Function

Rebecca Webber

"Brugger has accumulated evidence . . . that belief in paranormal activity is a brain function, just as emotion and cognition are."

In the following viewpoint writer Rebecca Webber features Peter Brugger. As a young man, Brugger considered himself a believer in the paranormal, particularly in the kind of unsettling coincidences he considered "meaningful." But when he became a doctoral student and began conducting research on issues of cognition and perception, Brugger began to change his mind about why people see patterns in phenomena rather than just accepting coincidences. This change in Brugger's own understanding of paranormal belief shaped not only his view of his personal history but also his ongoing research, which deals with the links between perception (the way people see things) and cognition (how the brain works).

Webber is a New York–based writer whose articles have appeared in *More*, *Real Simple*, *Pyschology Today*, and *Parade*. She is also a former senior reporter for *Glamour* magazine. She holds a master's degree from Columbia University's Graduate School of Journalism.

AS YOU READ, CONSIDER THE FOLLOWING QUESTIONS:
  1. According to Webber, what was the so-called meaningful coincidence that happened to Brugger as a young man in Zurich?
  2. What tools does the author say that Brugger uses in his ESP experiment?
  3. According to the author, what brain chemical does Brugger suspect plays a role in paranormal belief?

As a teenager, Peter Brugger vacuumed up information about the paranormal from books he found on his grandfather's shelves. "I was very interested in things like astral projection and ESP [extrasensory perception], and I was also fascinated by the controversy between those who believed and those who thought it was nonsense." Brugger counted himself among the former. "I didn't consider myself a sender or receiver of the paranormal, but I had a lot of so-called meaningful coincidences," he says. "Things happened that just couldn't be chance." When he was 23, and walking along the streets of Zurich, a city he lived near but rarely visited, Brugger became convinced he would run into a former coworker. A shadowy figure approached. "I was sure it would be him," says Brugger. It wasn't. But seconds later, he met the man he'd been thinking about. "I couldn't believe it! I even went back to check if I could have seen his image in the window glass," he says.

Brugger pursued a Ph.D. in biology and steered his research toward the phenomenon of perception. For his dissertation, he performed an ESP study on two groups of people: those who believed in the paranormal and those who did not. He exposed his subjects to a rapid sequence of light flashes, and made them believe that the stimuli contained dice faces. The paranormal enthusiasts were particularly unlikely to repeat the same guess for a die twice in a row. Brugger concluded

FAST FACT

Researcher Peter Brugger has shown that seeing ghosts or doppelgangers (doubles of living people) can be the result of damage to the brain's parietal lobes.

that those who have a hard time accepting that weird occurrences are purely due to chance tend to believe in the paranormal, because it is a way to explain the coincidences they naturally distrust. Those who believe that funny occurrences—such as two identical die rolls in a row—sometimes happen haphazardly don't need to blame unseen forces. It was then that Brugger stopped believing.

His Research: After 20-plus years of scientific exploration. Brugger has accumulated evidence to show that belief in paranormal activity is a brain function, just as emotion and cognition are. The brain chemical dopamine is an obvious suspect. "People with too much dopamine literally see things; they have suspicious thoughts. They see too many patterns in what is random," he explains. Parkinson's patients take dopamine to control their motor symptoms. "If you give them too much, they begin to see things like schizophrenics do," he points out.

Probabilities of Dice Combinations

Roll	Probability					
2	1/36					
3	2/36					
4	3/36					
5	4/36					
6	5/36					
7	6/36					
8	5/36					
9	4/36					
10	3/36					
11	2/36					
12	1/36					

Taken from: Dollar Dazzlers, "Craps: General Dice Probability." http://dollardazzlers.com/craps.php.

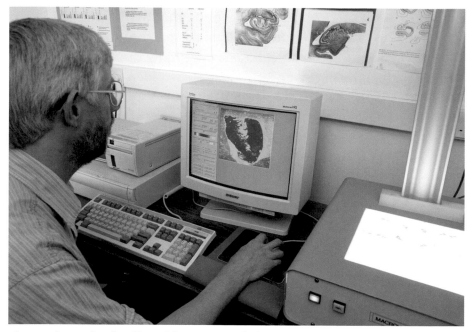

A researcher studies the effects of dopamine on the brain. Some researchers say evidence shows that belief in paranormal activity is a brain function, just as emotion and cognition are. The cause is thought to be linked to dopamine.

But the brain's role in one's belief system is much more complicated than that, he says. And his youthful wonder still manifests itself in his research. Based on an interest in out-of-body experiences, he's been exploring the phenomenon of phantom limbs. He discovered that patients register brain function in cortical areas when they "move" a phantom arm or leg, though not in the same areas that a person with limbs would activate if she were to imagine moving them.

EVALUATING THE AUTHOR'S ARGUMENTS:

In this viewpoint Rebecca Webber discusses a researcher who changed his opinion about paranormal phenomena based on a scientific experiment about chance and coincidence. Do you think scientific studies like this are more valid or convincing than firsthand experience? Why or why not?

Media and Culture Foster Belief in the Paranormal

Thomas De Zengotita

In this viewpoint Thomas De Zengotita, who is a media critic and journalist, considers why even very educated people are reluctant to deny outright the possibility that various paranormal phenomena and other unexplained events are possible. His argument is that we live in a culture in which complicated scientific concepts are not really understood except by a very small handful of people and in which the media does a poor job of explaining science in a meaningful or authoritative way. The result, he says, is that the public views all sorts of theories—scientifically sound and otherwise—as equally worthy of consideration and belief.

De Zengotita is a contributing editor to *Harper's* magazine and is on the faculty at New York University. He is the author of *Mediated: How the Media Shapes Your World and the Way You Live in It.*

"How could I be so arrogant and close-minded? How could I know that levitation wasn't possible?"

AS YOU READ, CONSIDER THE FOLLOWING QUESTIONS:
1. According to De Zengotita, what two explanations do guides at the Grand Canyon offer for the canyon's formation?
2. In the author's anecdote, what type of paranormal phenomenon prompted an argument between the author and two female friends?
3. What example does the author provide of a media metaphor that contributes to uncertainty and irrational beliefs?

A Vatican university is reviving its exorcism curriculum to confront burgeoning [growing] satanic cults in Italy, and a cardinal with close ties to the new pope recently backed away from the church's acceptance of evolution. Catholics can now line up with Protestant fundamentalists in the United States who are determined to get creationism into the biology curriculum because they believe in the Book of Genesis, literally. Fifty-two percent of Americans believe in astrology; 42 percent believe in communication with the dead. Forty-five percent believe in Noah's flood, and, when they visit the Grand Canyon these days, helicopter tour pilots accommodate them by describing, without judging either way, two accounts of the canyon's formation—one geological, the other being 40 days and 40 nights of rain.

Take your pick. It's a free country.

A lot of highly educated people find such developments pretty alarming, but if we want to understand what's really going on, we need to look past resurgent know-nothing movements. Try this. Take an informal little poll of a class of humanities students in any graduate school in the country. Ask how many believe in paranormal phenomena or alien abduction. If they feel free to respond honestly, the results won't be that different from what you would get if you polled an Oprah audience. They won't, for the most part, affirm a definite belief, but they won't want to issue any blanket denials either. Maybe, they will say, who knows? Who really knows anything?

A Story About Levitation
How did this situation come about? A little anecdote may shed some light.

The scene: a glorious summer day on Cape Cod, circa 1975. A dear friend of mine and her mother (lifelong bonds among all three of us) are sitting on a screened-in porch, sipping lemonade. They have just returned from a three-day retreat at an ashram in the Berkshires and are telling me all about it. I was curious about meditation. I knew it was correlated with measurable physiological effects, and I had heard a lot about it from trustworthy people—I was thinking I might try it. So I was listening with genuine interest. But it soon became apparent that this particular retreat had ventured way beyond meditation. Apparently, the Maharishi (the one who hung out with the Beatles) had achieved a breakthrough. He and his closest disciples at the central ashram (in Geneva, was it?) had embarked upon a radical new phase of enlightenment. They had achieved something very special, soon to be revealed to the world at a mass meditation event that would channel peace vibes across the planet. But some of these highly secret new techniques had been shared with the fortunate participants at this particular retreat in the Berkshires, by way of preparation for the big day.

Although there have been no conclusive scientific findings on paranormal-related levitation, many Americans believe it is possible. Additionally, 52 percent believe in astrology, and 42 percent think it is possible to communicate with the dead.

And what was this achievement, I asked?

Levitation.

I expressed a certain, ahhh, skepticism, shall we say? And they turned on me. These two extremely intelligent, Ivy League–educated women turned on me and proceeded to rake me over the coals with considerable vim. How could I be so arrogant and close-minded? How could I know that levitation wasn't possible?

As a general rule I make a practice of avoiding discussions of this kind; I smile and nod (no doubt a bit condescendingly) and wait for the subject to change. But this time I just snapped. I launched into a lecture on probability (I was reading a lot in philosophy of science at the time). I set up a scale to illustrate degrees of unlikelihood. At one extreme, logically impossible—a round square, given our definitions. Next, utterly, wildly unlikely, breaking established laws of physics at the Newtonian level—levitation. Next, very, very unlikely, given known laws—say, clairvoyance. And so on, through ESP and alien abduction and, toward the other end of the scale, I put the probability that Hitler and Eleanor Roosevelt were living together in Argentina.

All in vain. They believed.

Belief Is Powerful

Apparently they had been shown videotapes from the ashram in Geneva, and, though the tapes were rather grainy and shadowy for some reason, you could make out enough to tell that those yogis were . . . hovering.

Plus, my friends had practiced some of these techniques themselves in the Berkshires, don't forget, and, though they never actually got airborne, they could definitely feel themselves getting . . . lighter.

They wanted to believe. That's the key to this whole phenomenon, the thread to keep track of.

Exasperated, hoping to jolt them out of their post-retreat trance, I proposed a bet. Five hundred dollars each (a lot of money in those

> **FAST FACT**
>
> Maharishi Mahesh Yogi's followers claim that ten thousand people have learned the techniques of so-called Yogic Flying.

days, but I wasn't worried) that in two years levitation would be a universally acknowledged fact. Squadrons of levitating gurus floating down Fifth Avenue, on the Johnny Carson show, evidence like that.

And they took the bet!

Time passed, and no levitators materialized, but my dear friends were remarkably undisturbed. They weren't embarrassed into reassessing their worldview from the ground up, not at all, far from it. It was as if they had lost a bet on a sporting event. They had been wrong about the specifics on this one, but what did that prove? Maybe next time, who knows?

Who Really Knows Anything?

Who really knows anything?

Just recently I happened to tell one of my very best graduate students that story. I was chortling as I went along, confident that she would share my point of view, but as I reached the end of my tale I noticed a little frown on her face—and she said, guess what?

"How do you know levitation isn't possible?"

Then she told me about how she had once seen this dancer/acrobat who raised his whole body in the air on one finger.

Flabbergasted, I exclaimed, "But the finger was touching the floor, right?"

It didn't matter. Unusual balancing abilities and really strong fingers didn't interest her. She wanted to believe that this guy could have been on the way to levitating, at least.

She called me close-minded, too.

I asked her if she had studied science. Sure, and she'd done very well, as in all her studies. But it wasn't her thing. She didn't identify with it. What she most remembered, in fact, was that all those scientific theories eventually get disproved anyway—so, see?

Anything is possible. That she could identify with. . . .

Here's why.

Media Influences

Take the Science section of *The New York Times*, for example. Every other Tuesday or so, it carries a sort of (but not really) accessible description of dark matter or multiple universes or time-space foam or quantum strings that oscillate through 10 dimensions or whatever—you

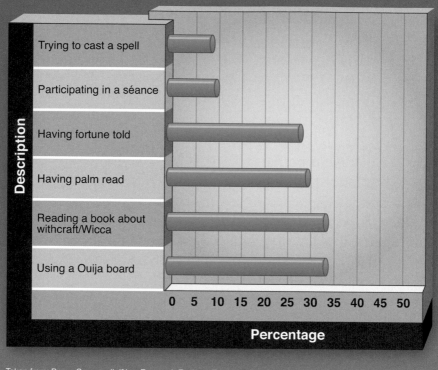

Percentage of Teens Who Have Experimented with the Supernatural

Description / Percentage

- Trying to cast a spell
- Participating in a séance
- Having fortune told
- Having palm read
- Reading a book about withcraft/Wicca
- Using a Ouija board

0 5 10 15 20 25 30 35 40 45 50

Percentage

Taken from: Barna Group poll, "New Research Explores Teenage Views and Behavior Regarding the Supernatural," January 23, 2006. www.barna.org/barna-update/article/5-barna-update/164-new-research-explores-teenage-views-and-behavior-regarding-the-supernatural?q=teenagers+teens.

know the kind of thing. But since you can't do the math on any of it, all you have to go on is the metaphors the grateful science writers borrow from the few hundred physicists in the world who can do the math.

But here's the thing. Those metaphors actually do seem to converge on the message that anything is possible. A recent one I recall concerned the in-principle possibility of time travel. I remember it so well because they chose to illustrate the main thesis (everything that ever happened or ever will happen is, at some theoretical level, always happening) by comparing the entirety of space-time to a really big loaf of bread. They splashed a drawing—in zany 1920s-cartoon style— across half a page, like a big old *Mad* magazine spread, very retro, lots of kooky detail. It showed the entirety of space-time as this loaf of bread, with slices falling away from each other slightly. A dinosaur was poking his head out of one slice, looking hilariously baffled. Some caveman—complete with leopard-skin toga and club—was peering out of a more "recent" slice with a question mark over his head.

Cute. Lots of mind-bending conundrums leavened with a few chuckles—that's the editorial recipe for these stories.

But consider. If you can't do the math, and all you understand about science you get from a steady diet of this kind of thing, then, over time, levitation is going to start to seem pretty tame, right?

EVALUATING THE AUTHOR'S ARGUMENTS:

Thomas De Zengotita suggests that even educated adults are unlikely to deny outright the possibility of various paranormal phenomena. He invites readers to poll graduate students to test this claim. Try a poll like this in your own classroom. What results do you obtain? How do the results of your own poll back up or conflict with the author's claims?

Viewpoint

5

Interest in the Paranormal May Be a Fad

Stephen Armstrong

"It might be appropriate to say that psychics are the new rock 'n' roll."

In the United Kingdom, colleges that offer coursework in psychic studies are thriving, thanks to a new generation of young enthusiasts in their twenties and thirties. According to Stephen Armstrong, the author of this viewpoint, the trend toward studying paranormal phenomena is part of a larger cultural fad, inspired by celebrities who claim to be psychic and by popular television programs that focus on psychic phenomena. The author suggests that these young people are turning toward the paranormal as a way to fill spiritual voids in their lives, much as they turn to fad diets and herbal remedies to help alleviate voids in other areas of their lives.

Armstrong is a journalist whose writing appears in a variety of publications, including *GQ, Elle, The Guardian,* and *The New Statesman.*

AS YOU READ, CONSIDER THE FOLLOWING QUESTIONS:

1. According to Armstrong, how do today's students of psychic phenomena differ from those in the past?
2. What does the author say are some of the most popular paranormal television series in the United Kingdom?
3. Armstrong says that Kay Stirling attributes the growing interest in psychic phenomena to the decreasing interest in what?

It's a hot evening and the west London traffic is moving at a slow, sweaty pace. Above it, in a scruffy attic room near the Natural History Museum, a small group of young women gathers to talk about life and death. One has funky dreadlocks piled high on her head, another is an earnest social worker from New Zealand who leans forward urgently when she talks, and a third—a marketing consultant—has the crisp enunciation of the very well educated. All in their twenties, they might be studying in adult education. And in a sense, they are.

The course they're on is called "Starting Your Spiritual Journey". One of these women wants to open her eyes to the spiritual world; one hopes to become a healer; and one—the social worker—wants to develop her psychic potential and use it at work to help the children she sees.

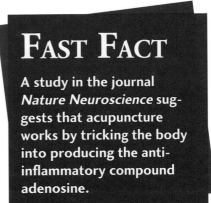

FAST FACT

A study in the journal *Nature Neuroscience* suggests that acupuncture works by tricking the body into producing the anti-inflammatory compound adenosine.

We are in the College of Psychic Studies, founded in 1884 by the spiritualist movement with support from [author] Arthur Conan Doyle, and in all its 122 years the place has never been busier. Ten years ago [1996], according to the "Spiritual Journey" tutor Kay Stirling, it was offering around 12 courses to a slow trickle of students. In the past few years, the trickle has swelled to a river.

A New Kind of Student

The college now offers more than 50 courses—all of them packed—called such things as "Psychic Beginnings", "Opening Psychic Sensitivity", "Heart Centred Soul Healing", "Intuitive Living for Success and Fulfilment", "Sensing Energy" and "First Steps as a Psychic and Medium". And it's not alone. In Essex, the Intuition Psychic Centre teaches tarot reading, psychic development and mediumship, while in Swansea the Academy of Psychic and Spiritual Studies offers lessons in mediumship training, spirit guides and angels. There are similar colleges in Winchester, Darlington, Leeds and Glasgow. All are booming—with a new kind of student.

The College of Psychic Studies in London, England, which offers courses on paranormal phenomena, has seen a huge increase in enrollment over the last decade, testifying to increased interest in the paranormal.

"Until about five years ago, most of the people interested in psychic phenomena were basically of a certain type," says Craig Hamilton-Parker, who runs the online Elysium Academy Psychic School, based in Stansted, and also practises as a medium. "You could call them the Doris Stokes [a famous psychic] brigade. They were usually over 50, might well have had a loved one who had died and were very keen to know what was on the other side. Over the past few years, however, we've had so much interest from people in their twenties or thirties who want to use skills such as aura reading, psychic abilities, mediumship and clairvoyance in their personal lives to help with relationships and careers and are unlikely to be wanting to contact and speak to the dead."

These students are part of a new, prosperous, younger generation whose desire for the psychic skills of mediumship and tarot reading sits comfortably alongside a range of other lifestyle choices, such as reading self-help books, going to the gym and dressing for success. Generation X-files, if you will. . . .

With [singer] Robbie Williams declaring himself "a little bit psychic" this year [2006], it might be appropriate to say that psychics are the new rock 'n' roll.

Psychic Television

This surge of interest has been encouraged by the gradual rise of psychic television. E4's big summer drama series—bought to play alongside *Big Brother*—has been *Ghost Whisperer*, starring Jennifer Love Hewitt as a pale and beautiful maverick who can see dead people. It joins ITV's *Supernatural*, a kind of *Ghostbusters*-meets-*Butch Cassidy and the Sundance Kid*, in which two brothers search for their dead father and deal with spooky small-town mysteries along the way. Most of all, though, the paranormal boom is probably down to Living TV, a satellite station aimed mainly at women, which is cited by many students at the College of Psychic Studies as their inspiration. . . .

In a sense, of course, it doesn't matter whether there actually is contact with the other side. This is the apotheosis [highest point] of the self-help generation. If we feel ill we turn to herbalists or homoeopaths. If we feel depressed, there's St John's wort or internet sites that will sell us happy pills without a prescription. If we're overweight, there's the Atkins diet. If we're tired, there are energy drinks. This is just another area of control.

The crumbling of politics and religion has helped spur the growth. Kay Stirling, the "Spiritual Journey" tutor, came to spiritualism via anti-Vietnam protests in Australia and radical feminism in the 1970s. "As the movement splintered, I became more interested in

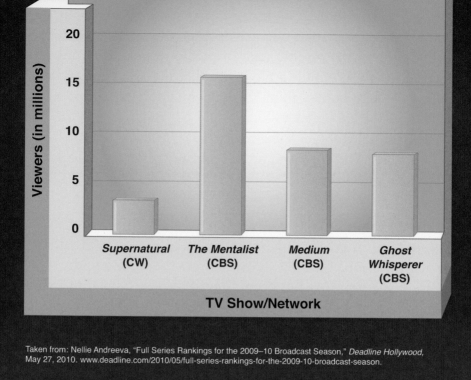

Taken from: Nellie Andreeva, "Full Series Rankings for the 2009–10 Broadcast Season," *Deadline Hollywood*, May 27, 2010. www.deadline.com/2010/05/full-series-rankings-for-the-2009-10-broadcast-season.

finding solutions in personal responsibility," she explains. "I think that drew me towards channelling my energy, and on into spiritualism. You'll find lots of people my age came through that route, but these younger kids are turning towards it because there's no sense of God in a world where people kill each other over religion the whole time."

Living TV's paranormal ratings back her up. On its main show, *Most Haunted*—now in its eighth series—mediums investigate hauntings in famous buildings. Almost half of the *Most Haunted* audience is aged 16–34, while only 7 per cent of those who watch BBC1's *Songs of Praise* are in that age group. Even in terms of numbers the spooky minority channel is gaining ground—the total *Songs of Praise* [featuring inspiring songs and stories] audience has halved since 2001, averaging under two million, while *Most Haunted* has more than half a million, despite being limited to multi-channel homes.

Of course, this may just be another fad. Perhaps in five years' time, Scientology will take over as the groovy route to the godhead. It's hard to predict. The only people who should know are the psychics themselves. After all, isn't that their job?

EVALUATING THE AUTHOR'S ARGUMENTS:

In this viewpoint Stephen Armstrong appears to credit the boom in popularity for courses in psychic studies to the popularity of television shows. What do you think? Are television shows about paranormal phenomena fueling a fad? Or are they reflecting one?

Chapter 3

Does Belief in Paranormal Phenomena Conflict with Religious Beliefs?

Many people believe that Jesus's ascent to heaven occurred by the hand of God. Others think it was accomplished through levitation. Some think there are events described in the Bible that seem paranormal in nature.

Belief in Psychic Phenomena Conflicts with Christian Beliefs

Oswin Craton

"Even God's prophets could know nothing of the future unless He revealed it to them."

In this viewpoint Oswin Craton, who writes from the perspective of a believer in the Christian faith, addresses the claims of modern-day prophets who say they have the ability to foresee the future. The author contrasts these psychics and fortune-tellers to Old Testament prophets in several ways, utilizing many references to the Bible to help make his arguments. According to the author, unless prophets receive their visions of the future directly from God (as opposed to from some special gift or talent that they possess), they are not really prophets at all. He encourages Christians to have high standards and to consider scriptural evidence as they evaluate the assertions of psychics and others who claim to see the future.

"Oswin Craton" is the pen name of American musician and composer John Craton. Writing as Oswin Craton, the author has published several online collections of writings on religion and has also written a book titled *A Journey of Fear and Joy*.

AS YOU READ, CONSIDER THE FOLLOWING QUESTIONS:
1. According to Craton, biblical prophets' gifts of foreseeing the future came from what source?
2. What does the author say is the first criterion for a true prophet of God?
3. In order for a prophet to be considered "true," the author says, what percentage of his or her predictions must be accurate?

Scripture tells us of various people throughout history who have been given the gift of prophecy, and I do believe the Bible. The ability to see into the future against the obstacle of time is a well-attested fact in Scripture, and I do not discount these claims in any fashion. But I do think it important to note some significant differences between biblical accounts of future-telling with many modern-day claims. Let us examine some of these differences.

Old Testament Prophecy

When we read the books of prophecy in the Old Testament we find a consistent claim running through them all. Summarized succinctly, that claim is "The word of the Lord came." Biblical prophecy is generally defined as a foretelling of future events by means of divine revelation. That means the prophet knew of future events because God revealed them to him in some way. There is no claim by any of the biblical prophets that they possessed any particular gift of their own. This is made particularly clear in Daniel 2:27–30 where Daniel tells King Nebuchadnezzar that while he himself is unable to divine the king's message, "There is a God in heaven that revealeth secrets." Such claims are repeated over and over by the Old Testament prophets. They laid no claim to having any special "gift" but in all cases said it was God who revealed these things to them. They did not resort to magic or any "secret knowledge" hidden from the common man. In

Daniel's case it was the Chaldeans who claimed such superior abilities for themselves, but they were unable to discern either the king's dream or its interpretation. The ability (if we want to call it that) came directly from God and only as He ordained. Even God's prophets could know nothing of the future unless He revealed it to them.

How does this differ from those today who claim the gift of precognition [the ability to see the future]? Those who claim to possess ESP [extrasensory perception] which allows them to see the future believe their special ability comes from *within themselves*. While some profess to have the talent as a gift from God, they usually do not say that God actually tells them these things beforehand or that God speaks to them in any divine way. The prophets of old did.

In the Old Testament Daniel (kneeling) tells King Nebuchadnezzar that he is unable to divine the King's message but that "there is a God in heaven that revealeth secrets." Prophets throughout the Bible speak of God revealing things only to them.

False Prophets

But what of those today who do claim the same type of prophecy for themselves as those found in Scripture? Let's first look at the criteria Scripture lays down for a prophet. Deuteronomy 13:1–4 says:

> If there arise among you a prophet, or a dreamer of dreams, and giveth thee a sign or a wonder, and the sign or the wonder come to pass, whereof he spake unto thee, saying, Let us go after other gods, which thou hast not known, and let us serve them; thou shalt not hearken unto the words of that prophet, or that dreamer of dreams: for the Lord your God proveth you, to know whether ye love the Lord your God with all your heart and with all your soul. Ye shall walk after the Lord your God, and fear him, and keep his commandments, and obey his voice, and ye shall serve him, and cleave unto him.

Deuteronomy 18:21–22 offer a further criterion: "And if thou say in thine heart, How shall we know the word which the Lord hath not spoken, when a prophet speaketh in the name of the Lord, if the thing follow not, nor come to pass, that is the thing which the Lord hath not spoken, but the prophet hath spoken it presumptuously: thou shalt not be afraid of him."

FAST FACT

The so-called Jeane Dixon effect is the tendency of the media to spotlight a psychic's few correct predictions and ignore his or her many incorrect ones.

Tests of the True Prophets

These are the two main criteria Scripture gives for determining whether a person who claims to be a prophet of God is genuine. The first is that the true prophet will not lead the people to serve other gods. In this case, even if what he says comes true, if he subsequently leads his hearers away from God he is a false prophet. (We might cite the example of Jeane Dixon who claimed to be a modern-day prophet. Some of her predictions—though relatively few—were in fact accurate, and she gained many followers during her lifetime. But she led many of her followers into astrology and occultism, violating the first sign of a true prophet.) The second criterion is that

Old Testament Prophets

Amos	Daniel	Ezekiel
Habakkuk	Haggai	Hosea
Isaiah	Jeremiah	Joel
Jonah	Malachi	Micah
Nahum	Obadiah	Zechariah
Zephaniah		

Taken from: Paul R. Schmidtbleicher, "A Basic Overview of the Bible: Part I, Old Testament," 2000. http://scriptureman.com.

whenever a prophet predicts an event that does not come to pass, then he is a false prophet. This would not simply include the "general" predictions which nearly anyone could foresee (such as "a famous movie star will come out of the closet this year"), but would mean that he should be able to predict something precisely and accurately. And according to this criterion, what should be the prophet's prediction rate? The latter passage does not say that the prophet should be believed if 50% of what his predictions come true, or if 80% or even 99% of his prophecies are validated. It is a blanket statement. *All* of his predictions must be accurate—100%. If his accuracy rate falls below that standard, he is not to be feared or believed. For a modern-day prophet to be determined genuine, he must first never lead anyone away from God and must furthermore be 100% correct in every prophecy he utters. Many "professional psychics" are hailed for their ability to have a 75% accuracy rate (and factored into those are statements like the one above which anyone could make). As Christians, our standard is much higher.

EVALUATING THE AUTHOR'S ARGUMENTS:

Oswin Craton uses Old Testament scripture almost entirely as the evidence for his arguments. How well do you think this technique might work for an audience of Christians? Non-Christians? Explain your answers.

There Is a Close Relationship Between Paranormal and Religious Experiences

Hugh Montefiore

"There is clearly some connection between religion and the paranormal, but it is difficult to discover exactly what it is."

In this viewpoint Hugh Montefiore suggests that many accounts of miraculous events in the lives of Christian saints resemble other accounts of paranormal phenomena. He explores anecdotes of three phenomena—stigmata, incense, and levitation—to provide examples of the kinds of paranormal experiences that might indicate holiness, devotion, or a close relationship with God. He provides accounts of the lives of St. Francis of Assisi and St. Teresa of Avila, in particular. In addition to these detailed examples, the author also lists several other unexplained phenomena that arise in the stories of saints' lives. Christians, the author says, might view these occurrences as miracles proving God's existence; others might view them as evidence of other mystical forces or as a result of religious hysteria.

Montefiore was the bishop of Birmingham in the United Kingdom from 1977 to 1987 and has authored several books, including *The Paranormal: A Bishop Investigates.*

AS YOU READ, CONSIDER THE FOLLOWING QUESTIONS:
1. What does Montefiore say is the definition of "stigmata"?
2. Which saint famously levitated, as described by the author?
3. According to Montefiore, what is a possible explanation for "an odor of sanctity"?

When events occur or phenomena take place which are inexplicable in scientific terms, they are called 'paranormal' or 'psi effects'. Scientists often prefer to call them 'anomalies' because it is difficult for them to accept that some things cannot be explained scientifically.

Some scientists discount the paranormal for the same reason that they reject religion: they believe, as a matter of faith, that the material universe, with its laws of cause and effect, accounts for everything. Most objections, however, concern the scientific method. One of the ways in which scientific explanations are tested is by repetition. But paranormal phenomena generally happen spontaneously, so there is no way they can be replicated. A further problem is that, in scientific experiments, the effect is the same whoever is carrying out an experiment, but some people seem to be able to produce paranormal effects while others cannot. However, the evidence suggests that such events do occur. What's more, they have been critically and carefully examined ever since 1882, when a Cambridge University professor inaugurated the Society for Psychical Research, which is still going strong today. Paranormal events cover a large range of phenomena, such as telepathy, clairvoyance, precognition and dowsing [the art of finding hidden objects]. They also include the work of mediums, automatic writing, psycho-kinesis (objects which move for no apparent reason), apparitions and hauntings.

Paranormal phenomena which are associated with religion include poltergeist activities, psychic imprints on a local environment,

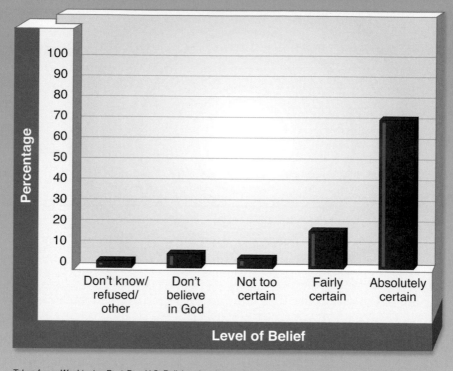

Belief in God or a Higher Power

Level of Belief

Taken from: *Washington Post*, Pew U.S. Religious Landscape Survey, 2008. www.washingtonpost.com/wp-dyn/content/graphic/2008/06/23/GR2008062301409.htm?sid=ST2008062300818&s_pos=list.

earthbound spirits, cleansing of a polluted environment and, in extreme cases, exorcism (casting out evil spirits). . . .

There is clearly some connection between religion and the paranormal, but it is difficult to discover exactly what it is. They are not identical, nor does it follow that a saint will be the subject of paranormal phenomena. Certainly such phenomena do not in themselves point to sanctity [holiness]. On the other hand, these strange phenomena have been connected with saintly people, and evidence about these phenomena is often more reliable than that about other kinds of paranormal events because it has been given on oath (such as is required in the Roman Catholic Church for candidates for sainthood). The saints and mystics to whom the experiences occur wish to keep them private and do not regard them as important in their search for unity with God.

There are many of these phenomena. They include prolonged tasting, experiencing great heat, transfiguration with bright light, extraordinary healings and incorruption [failure to decay] of the body after death.

Stigmata

Stigmata describe the appearance of mysterious wounds (often with bleeding) on a person's hands and feet corresponding to the places where Christ was believed to have been wounded on the cross. In fact, Christ's wounds were not in his hands (which could not have born the weight of his body). Paul wrote 'I bear in my body the

marks of the Lord Jesus' (Galatians 6:17). Unless this refers to the stigmata, the first person to receive them was probably St Francis of Assisi in the thirteenth century. Brother Leo wrote within 2 to 5 years of his death:

> The blessed Francis, two years before his death, kept a Lent in the hermitage of the Alverna. . . . After the vision and speech he had with a seraph [a type of angel] and the impression on his body of the stigmata of Christ, he made these praises. . . .

Since then hundreds of cases have been reported, but only about 50 have been sufficiently documented. Usually the recipients were people of great devotion and piety, although some had earlier shown symptoms of neurotic disorder. Except for St Francis and two others (one of them, known as Padre Pio, lived in the twentieth century), those with the stigmata have been women. Stigmata are associated with ecstasy. Some regard them as the product of hysteria (using the term in its extended medical usage), but this does not explain how they appear. The stigmata are extraordinary signs of devotion to Christ, the result of deep meditation on his Passion.

The first known stigmata were those of Francis of Assisi, said to have been placed on his body by an angel. The stigmata represent the wounds on the body of the crucified Christ.

Incense

Since early times, a fragrance-like incense has been experienced from saintly people. It was noted in the martyrdom of Polycarp in the second century. Gregory the Great in the sixth century wrote about an acquaintance from whom there came a 'pleasant and fragrant smell' after his death. There are many other well-authenticated cases. Three medical doctors made a deposition about the strong odour of primroses which emanated from a Carmelite nun's dead body. In the sixteenth century St Teresa of Avila recounted what her nuns told her about the visit of a particularly holy lady: 'The nearer they came to her, the sweeter it was, though her dress was of such a kind that, in the heat, which was very severe, one could have expected its odour to be offensive.' Strange fragrances have also been noted in the very different circumstances of a mediumistic seance.

Levitation

Levitation—when a person finds himself or herself lifted from the ground involuntarily—is another phenomenon shown by some of the saints which has also been found among those with paranormal gifts. It cannot be explained by any natural process. St Teresa of Avila (among many others) provides a good example. She found it so embarrassing that she begged God to stop these visible favours. On one occasion she had to be held down by her nuns! After her death a nun swore on oath that she had put her hands beneath Teresa's body when she had been lifted up for half an hour in an ecstasy, but Teresa had been forbidden to speak of this in her lifetime.

Are There Any Explanations for These Phenomena?

These three phenomena are possibly psychosomatic [caused by mental factors] in origin. Stigmata may be the outward manifestation of an inner identity with and devotion to Jesus. The odour of sanctity may be the external sign of a sweetness of soul. Levitation may be a visible embodiment of the soul soaring to God. No one can explain how or to whom they occur.

EVALUATING THE AUTHOR'S ARGUMENTS:

Hugh Montefiore suggests that evidence of paranormal phenomena given about saints and other holy people is more reliable than general accounts because it is given under oath. Do you find the examples the author provides convincing? Why or why not?

Viewpoint

3

Religion and the Paranormal Should Be Studied Side by Side

Mark Oppenheimer

"Dr. Kripal is different, because he is sympathetic to the possibility that the paranormal may be real—not just the product of people's false perceptions."

In the following viewpoint Mark Oppenheimer profiles Jeffrey J. Kripal, a scholar who believes that paranormal phenomena should be studied seriously—but not necessarily as science. Instead, Kripal, who is a specialist in religious studies, believes that scholars of religion should consider accounts of unexplained phenomena such as telepathy, alien abductions, and near-death experiences alongside more "accepted" accounts of miracles and other seemingly supernatural events that are accepted components of mainstream religions. Kripal, who acknowledges that he himself has had mystical experiences, believes that accounts of paranormal phenomena should be taken seriously by students of religions and not dismissed or belittled.

Oppenheimer is a lecturer in the English and political science departments at Yale University and is the director of the Yale

Journalism Initiative. He holds a doctorate in religious studies and writes a biweekly column about religion for *The New York Times*. He is the author of three books, most recently *Wisenheimer: A Childhood Subject to Debate.*

AS YOU READ, CONSIDER THE FOLLOWING QUESTIONS:
1. According to Oppenheimer, French ufologist Jacques Vallee inspired the main character in what Steven Spielberg movie?
2. Where was Kripal, according to the author, when he had his life-changing spiritual experience?
3. What does the author say is the topic of Kripal's next book?

Practically anything goes at the American Academy of Religion's annual conference, where scholars of dozens of religions convene annually to debate, relate and on occasion mate. Conversation ranges from the Talmud [Jewish law] to tantra [a Hindu Buddhist text], from Platonism to Satanism. In 2010, from Oct. 30 to Nov. 1 in Atlanta, nearly 5,000 people attended panels including "Seeking New Meanings of God and Dao" and "Madness, Smallpox, and Death in Tibet."

What was almost impossible to find, at this orgy of intellectual curiosities, was discussion of the paranormal: ESP, premonitions, psychic powers, alien abduction and the like. This is a conference concerned with all sorts of supernatural and metaphysical claims. In panels, over coffee and during cocktail-hour quarrels, they talk of Moses at the burning bush, the virgin birth, Muhammad's journey on a winged horse. So why nothing about, say, mental telepathy?

That is the question posed by Jeffrey J. Kripal, a professor of religion at Rice University in Houston and a renegade advocate for including the paranormal in religious studies. In his new book, *Authors of the Impossible: The Paranormal and the Sacred* he tries to convince serious religion scholars that they ought to study, say, ESP or alien abduction.

From Spirituality to the Supernatural

Most scholars study traditions even nonbelievers are comfortable talking about, like Judaism and Christianity. And a growing number study

اختلاف ید رد بعض ملائكه صورتلری و براق شكلی بونلرد زكه تحریر قلندی
تایعجا صنع باری تعالی مشاهدت قلنه كه ننك كبی خوصوصلرد صانعه رفتارك الله الحسب

This sixteenth-century Turkish manuscript shows angels and the mythical winged horse Buraq, who carried Muhammad on his ascent to heaven. Paranormal researchers say religious incidents of this kind should be discussed as paranormal-related events.

kinds of "spirituality": the belief in guardian angels, for example, or in an invisible force, not specific to a major religion.

But Dr. Kripal wants to go further, into supernaturalism that seems bizarre to most Westerners. His book is about four pre-eminent writers on the paranormal: the 19th-century psychical researcher Frederic Myers; Charles Fort, who died in 1932; the contemporary French ufologist [someone who studies UFOs] Jacques Vallee, who inspired the character Claude Lacombe in "Close Encounters of the Third Kind"; and his fellow ufologist Bertrand Méheust. None are widely studied, but Dr. Kripal says all prove that one can write in a sophisticated way about the paranormal.

According to Dr. Kripal, their omission is evidence of a persistent bias among religion scholars, happy to consider the inexplicable, like miracles, as long as they fit a familiar narrative, like Judaism or Christianity.

"There is resistance in the way our universities are set up, in the elite culture of higher education," says Dr. Kripal, 48, who grew up in Nebraska and once planned to be a Benedictine monk. "Paranormal events completely violate the epistemologies [theories of belief or knowledge] around which we have formed our own knowledge.

Blurring Boundaries

"The sciences study objects and use mechanistic [physical] cause models to track them. The humanities specialize in subjectivity, meaning, consciousness, art, religion. Paranormal events violate that division. They clearly involve human subjectivity, and they clearly involve objects out there."

In other words, it is one thing to study a miracle a thousand years old—that seems a safe question for the historian or the theologian. But what to do with people who say they were abducted by a U.F.O. last week?

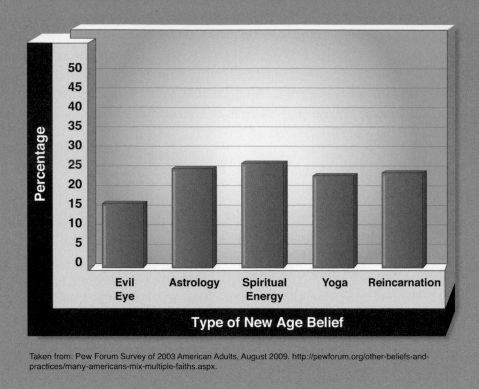

Percentage of Americans Who Follow New Age Beliefs

Taken from: Pew Forum Survey of 2003 American Adults, August 2009. http://pewforum.org/other-beliefs-and-practices/many-americans-mix-multiple-faiths.aspx.

"The easiest way to deal with them is to dismiss them, or humiliate them, or claim they are fraudulent, or mistaken," Dr. Kripal says. "That allows us to preserve our forms of knowledge. For not only do they violate the sciences and humanities, they also violate orthodox forms of religion, which often want to read these things"—like speaking with the dead or reading minds—"as demonic."

Leaning Toward the Paranormal

Ann Taves, a past president of the American Academy of Religion, says that other scholars are interested in esoteric religion outside the major traditions, but that Dr. Kripal is different, because he is sympathetic to the possibility that the paranormal may be real—not just the product of people's false perceptions.

"Jeff brings certain metaphysical [outside the laws of nature] commitments or leanings to the study that gives his work a certain intensity," Ms. Taves says. "Some of the rest of us consider these kinds of claims like other religious and metaphysical claims. We don't lean toward the metaphysical claims—we distance ourselves from that."

And she is right: Dr. Kripal "leans toward" the paranormal—he does not dismiss it as the fruit of deluded minds. He thinks there is some external reality being talked about, something real out there. In this regard, he is like the four mystics he writes about in *Authors of the Impossible.* In a previous book, *Roads of Excess, Palaces of Wisdom: Eroticism and Reflexivity in the Study of Mysticism*, Dr. Kripal discusses a mystical experience of his own, in 1989, in India. He describes being asleep one night: "Suddenly, without warning, a powerful electric-like energy flooded the body with wave after wave of an unusually deep and uniform arousal. I watched my legs and torso float uncontrollably towards the ceiling."

Dr. Kripal says that night prepared him, in a way, to encounter his four *Authors of the Impossible*—like Mr. Vallee, whose 1969 book, *Passport to Magonia*, places flying saucers in a tradition that includes elves, fairies, sylphs and leprechauns.

"I suppose I've come to the conclusion," Dr. Kripal says, "that one of the functions of those earlier experiences I have written about was so that I could write these books." He is referring in part to his next book, to be published in 2011, about the paranormal experiences of the artists and authors of superhero comics.

What his fellow academics will make of that book, only someone with telepathic powers—Professor X of the X-Men, perhaps?—could tell us for sure.

EVALUATING THE AUTHOR'S ARGUMENTS:

One of the points made by Mark Oppenheimer in this viewpoint is that paranormal phenomena are not easily classified as belonging either to the sciences or to the humanities. What do you think? Which academic departments, if any, should include the study of paranormal phenomena in their coursework?

Near-Death Experiences May Prove the Existence of the Soul

Danny Penman

"People see the pain and suffering of dying and equate that with death— but they're not the same. Death is the progression of life."

According to Danny Penman, so-called near-death experiences—the accounts of people who have come close to death and then been resuscitated—share certain common elements. Penman provides an account of one such survivor and then discusses the work of a UK researcher who has investigated the possible continuation of human consciousness even after the body has been declared clinically dead.

Penman has a PhD in biochemistry from Liverpool University and is now a London-based investigative journalist specializing in issues of science, health, animal rights, and the environment.

AS YOU READ, CONSIDER THE FOLLOWING QUESTIONS:

1. According to Penman, whose voice did Jeanette Atkinson hear during her near-death experience?

2. What does the author say is the medical nickname for someone who is unconscious with no brain activity, pulse, or breathing?
3. How many of the sixty-three cardiac arrest sufferers that Dr. Parnia interviewed had had a near-death experience, according to the author?

Jeanette Atkinson is surprisingly relaxed about the time she died and went to the edge of heaven.

"I do not want to die again in the near future because I still have too much to do," she says. "But I have no fear of death. People see the pain and suffering of dying and equate that with death—but they're not the same. Death is the progression of life."

Jeanette, a 43-year-old student nurse from Eastbourne, had a near-death experience in 1979 when she was just 18 years old. It was triggered when a blood clot in her leg broke up into seven pieces and clogged the main vessels in her lungs, starving her body of oxygen. The doctors were certain that she would die. She did—but then returned to tell the tale.

"The first thing I noticed was that the world changed," says Jeanette.

The light became softer but clearer. Suddenly there was no pain. All I could see was my body from the chest downwards and I noticed that the time was 9:00pm. In an instant I found myself looking at the ceiling. It was only a few inches away. I remember thinking it was about time they cleaned the dust from the striplights! I then went on a little journey around the ward and along the corridor to see what the nurses were up to. One was writing on a notepad. It never occurred to me that I was dying. It was a lovely experience and very, very serene.

Toward the Light

Jeanette then began the journey that many others before her have reported—being drawn into a long dark tunnel suffused with light. "Everything went fuzzy," she says. "I found myself being drawn into a tunnel shaped like a corkscrew.

All I wanted to do was reach the beautiful lights at the bottom. The longing was so powerful but so gentle. I knew I desperately wanted to be there. But then a voice bellowed at me: 'Come on you silly old cow it's not your time yet!' I then shot back into my body—it's all a little unclear—all I can say is that I remember seeing the clock again and it was 9:20 P.M. The next thing I was aware of was waking up a few days later, surrounded by equipment and feeling terrible. Later on I realised that the voice I'd heard was my grandmother's. She'd died when I was three years old.

For decades near-death experiences like Jeanette's have been written off as delusions by scientists. They are dismissed as no more than the last twitches of a dying brain. Modern science has no place for mysticism and the paranormal. But now a group of British researchers are challenging the scientific establishment by launching a major study into near-death experiences. They hope to settle once and for all the question of whether there truly is life after death.

Many people liken a near-death experience to traveling down a long, dark tunnel toward a distant light.

New Technology

"We now have the technology and scientific knowledge to begin exploring the ultimate question," says Dr Sam Parnia, leader of the research team at London's Hammersmith Hospital. "To be honest, I started off as a sceptic but having weighed up all the evidence I now think that there is something going on. It's not possible to talk in terms of 'life after death'. In scientific terms we can only say that there is now evidence that consciousness may carry on after clinical death. Our work will prove one way or the other whether a form of consciousness carries on after the body and brain has died."

Several scientific studies have suggested that the mind—or 'soul'—lives on after the body has died and the brain ceased to function. One study published in the prestigious *Lancet* medical journal found that one in ten cardiac arrest survivors experienced emotions, visions or lucid thoughts while they were clinically dead. In medical terms they were 'flatliners' or unconscious with no signs of brain activity, pulse or breathing.

> **FAST FACT**
>
> An ongoing, multiyear study at twenty-five hospitals in the United Kingdom and United States is testing whether survivors have out-of-body experiences during cardiac arrest episodes.

Common Experiences

About one in four people who have a near-death experience also have a much more profound—and sometimes disturbing—experience such as watching doctors try and resuscitate their bodies. These 'out-of-body experiences' often include seeing a bright light, traveling down a tunnel, seeing their dead body from above, and meeting deceased relatives.

Research in America has uncovered even more bizarre results. Blind people who underwent near-death experiences were able to see whilst they were 'dead'—even those who had been blind from birth. They did not experience perfect vision, often it was out of focus or hazy, as if they were seeing the world for the first time through a thin mist. But the vision was sufficiently clear for them to watch doctors trying to resuscitate their clinically dead bodies.

Common Near-Death Experiences Among Sixty-Two Cardiac-Arrest Patients

Experience	Number	Percentage
Awareness of being dead	31	50%
Positive emotions	35	56%
Out-of-body experience	15	24%
Moving through a tunnel	19	31%
Communication with light	14	23%
Observation of colors	14	23%
Observation of a celestial landscape	18	29%
Meeting with deceased persons	20	32%
Life review	8	13%
Presence of border	5	8%

Reprinted from *The Lancet*, vol. 358, no. 9298, Pirn van Lommel, Ruud van Wees, Vincent Meyers, Ingrid Elfferich, "Table 2: Frequency of Ten Elements of NDE, in Near-Death Experiences in Survivors of Cardiac Arrest; A Prospective Study in the Netherlands," p. 2041. Copyright © 2001, with permission from Elsevier.

Dr Parnia has previously studied near-death experiences. Two years ago his work was published in the prestigious medical journal *Resuscitation*. Dr Parnia's team rigorously interviewed 63 cardiac arrest patients and discovered that seven had memories of their brief period of 'death', although only four passed the Greyson scale, the strict medical criteria for assessing near-death experiences. These four recounted feelings of peace and joy, they lost awareness of their own bodies, time speeded up, they saw a bright light and entered another world, encountered a mystical being and faced a 'point of no return'.

According to modern medicine all of these patients were effectively dead. Their brains had shut down and no thoughts or feelings were possible. There was certainly no possibility of the complex brain activity required for dreaming or hallucinating. . . .

Believers

But all of the theories and questions posed by scientists are academic to those who have had a near-death experience. They know the answers.

"There is no doubt in my mind that there's life after death because I've seen the other side," says Jeanette. "I don't believe in a benevolent God. I've seen too much suffering for that but I'm very spiritual. I saw my daughter suffer for four years with cancer. She died when she was only 17. I know she has gone to a better place."

EVALUATING THE AUTHOR'S ARGUMENTS:

Danny Penman seems to suggest that what scientists label "consciousness" or "the mind" is the same as the religious or spiritual concept of the "soul." Do you think this conclusion can be drawn based on the evidence provided in this viewpoint? Explain your answer.

Facts About Paranormal Phenomena

Editor's note: These facts can be used in reports or papers to reinforce or add credibility when making important points or claims.

Clairvoyance
- Clairvoyance is often called the "sixth sense" or "second sight."
- The term *clairvoyance* comes from the French *clair* (clear) and *voyance* (vision).

Extrasensory Perception (ESP)
- A 1979 survey indicated that two-thirds of college and university professors believed in ESP.
- A Japanese researcher claims to be able to communicate with a cactus and to have taught it to count and add up to twenty.
- In a 1987 University of Chicago survey, 67 percent of adults surveyed believed they had had at least one ESP experience.

Near-Death Experiences
According to the Near-Death Experience Research Foundation:
- The earliest known description of a near-death experience is in Plato's *Republic*, from 420 BC.
- The term *near-death experience* was coined by physician-philosopher Raymond Moody in 1975 in his book *Life After Life*.
- Each day 774 near-death experiences occur in the United States.

Parapsychology
- The term *parapsychology* was coined in the late nineteenth century by philosopher Max Dessoir.
- The term *parapsychology* comes from the Greek word meaning "alongside psychology."
- The first organization created to standardize psychical research was the British Society for Psychical Research, founded in 1882.

- Joseph Banks Rhine is recognized as the founder of modern scientific parapsychology. He founded a noted research lab at Duke University.

Psychokinesis
- The term *telekinesis,* an older word for *psychokinesis,* was first used by German-Russian researcher Alexander Asakof around 1890.
- Uri Geller, the most famous practitioner of psychokinesis, was unable to bend spoons on a 1973 appearance on *The Tonight Show Starring Johnny Carson* when Carson preselected the tableware.
- Geller claims to have been contacted by NASA to help "unstick" an antenna on the Galileo space probe using the power of his mind.

Telepathy
- *Telepathy* is derived from the Greek words *tele* (distant) and *pathe* (occurrence, or feeling).
- The aboriginal peoples of Australia accept telepathy as a normal human ability.
- Sigmund Freud was concerned that public acknowledgment of telepathy would cast doubt on the new field of psychoanalysis, but he believed that he had communicated remotely with his fiancée when he was in Paris.

Glossary

astral projection: A type of out-of-body experience that includes an "astral body" that exists separately from the physical body and is capable of traveling outside it.

clairvoyance: The ability to perceive things or events in the future, outside of the normal senses.

extrasensory perception (ESP): The reception of information through means other than the physical five senses.

functional magnetic resonance imaging (fMRI): A specialized type of magnetic scanning that measures change in blood flow related to neural activity in the brain and nervous system.

out-of-body experience: An experience that involves the sensation of traveling outside one's physical body.

parapsychology: The study of mental phenomena that fall outside of, or are unexplained by, standard scientific psychology.

precognition: Knowledge of an event before it occurs.

synchronicity: Simultaneous events that are causally unrelated or unlikely to occur together by pure chance but that seem to occur together in a meaningful manner.

telekinesis: The ability to move objects at a distance with mental power.

telepathy: The communication of ideas or thoughts by means other than the known senses.

Organizations to Contact

The editors have compiled the following list of organizations concerned with the issues debated in this book. The descriptions are derived from materials provided by the organizations. All have publications or information available for interested readers. The list was compiled on the date of publication of the present volume; the information provided here may change. Be aware that many organizations take several weeks or longer to respond to inquiries, so allow as much time as possible for the receipt of requested materials.

American Institute of Parapsychology
4131 NW Thirteenth St., Ste. 208
Gainesville, FL 32609
e-mail: anichols@gru.net
website: parapsychologylab.com

The American Institute of Parapsychology is a nonprofit research and educational institution that sponsors courses, research, and information on parapsychology. It also offers information and counseling for individuals who have experienced paranormal phenomena and serves as a resource for students and media representatives looking for information on these topics. Its website includes current scholarly articles.

American Society for Psychical Research (ASPR)
5 W. Seventy-Third St.
New York, NY 10023
(212) 799-5050
fax: (212) 496-2497
e-mail: aspr@aspr.com
website: www.aspr.com

Founded in 1885 by a group of scholars including William James, the ASPR is the oldest organization of its kind in the United States. Sigmund Freud and Carl Jung were honorary members in the society's early years. The society's library and archives provide an extensive history of paranormal research. It also supports ongoing research and publishes *The Journal of the American Society for Psychical Research.*

Committee for Skeptical Inquiry (CSI)
PO Box 703
Amherst, NY 14226
(716) 636-1425
e-mail: info@csicop.org
website: www.csicop.org

The CSI's mission is to examine controversial and extraordinary claims and to promote scientific inquiry and critical investigation. To that end, it encourages research that carefully examines claims of the paranormal, publishes articles on these topics, and sponsors meetings and networking. It also supports resources and education for young people to promote scientific methodologies and to combat superstition. Its primary publication is the journal *Skeptical Inquirer,* published six times per year.

James Randi Educational Foundation (JREF)
2941 Fairview Park Dr., Ste. 105
Falls Church, VA 22042
(703) 226-3780
fax: (703) 226-3781
website: www.randi.org

Founded in 1996 by magician and skeptic James Randi, the JREF promotes critical thinking and scientific investigation of psychic claims. The foundation offers a $1 million prize to anyone who scientifically demonstrates psychic, supernatural, or paranormal ability. To date, the prize has never been awarded. The foundation sponsors an annual Amazing Meeting and posts video presentations from the meeting and other events on its website.

Koestler Parapsychology Unit (KPU)
School of Philosophy, Psychology and Language Sciences, University of Edinburgh
7 George Sq.
Edinburgh EH8 9JZ, UK
+44 131 650 3440
fax: +44 131 650 3461

e-mail: Caroline.Watt@ed.ac.uk
website: www.koestler-parapsychology.psy.ed.ac.uk

The KPU, founded in 1985, is a research group based in the psychology department at the University of Edinburgh in Scotland. Its staff and students study various aspects of parapsychology, including the existence of psychic abilities, belief in the paranormal, and the history of parapsychology. Its website includes profiles of researchers and descriptions of current research projects.

Parapsychological Association (PA)
PO Box 24173
Columbus, OH 43224
e-mail: business@parapsych.org
website: www.parapsych.org

The PA is the professional organization of scientists and scholars worldwide engaged in the study of psychic experiences. It is an affiliate of the American Academy of Arts and Sciences and holds an annual convention. Its website includes extensive links to research labs, books, and current online experiments.

Parapsychology Foundation (PF)
PO Box 1562
New York, NY 10021
(212) 628-1550
fax: (212) 628-1559
website: www.parapsychology.org

The PF is a nonprofit foundation that supports scientific research into paranormal phenomena. The foundation offers grants and maintains a comprehensive library of more than twelve thousand books and periodicals about parapsychology and related topics. The organization also publishes a series of books and pamphlets about these topics, as well as the *International Journal of Parapsychology*.

PSI Research Centre
14 Selwood Rd.
Glastonbury
Somerset BA6 8HN, UK
e-mail: serena@psi-researchcentre.co.uk
website: www.psi-researchcentre.co.uk

The PSI Research Centre was founded by Serena Roney-Dougal, one of only fifty people in the United Kingdom to have obtained a PhD in parapsychological topics. The centre sponsors regular lectures and workshops on paranormal topics and has published many books and articles, including *The Faery Faith: An Integration of Science with Spirit* and *Where Science and Magic Meet.*

The Skeptics Society
PO Box 338
Altadena, CA 91001
(626) 794-3119
fax: (626) 794-1301
e-mail: skepticssociety@skeptic.com
website: www.skeptic.com

The Skeptics Society is intended to serve as an educational research source for people interested in investigating extraordinary claims of psychic phenomena. Its members include historians, scholars, scientists, magicians, educators, and others who are interested in the scientific exploration of controversial or extraordinary claims. The society publishes the quarterly journal *Skeptic* and a weekly e-newsletter, *eSkeptic.* It also sponsors a monthly lecture series and an annual conference.

Society for Psychical Research (SPR)
49 Marloes Rd.
Kensington, London W8 6LA UK
+44 207 9378984
website: www.spr.ac.uk

The SPR was established in 1882 and was the first organization created to use scientific principles to examine paranormal phenomena. It sponsors lectures and other events and publishes both the scholarly *Journal of the Society for Psychical Research* and the quarterly magazine *Paranormal Review.* Its website includes many links to research projects sponsored by the SPR and its members.

Society for Scientific Exploration (SSE)
PO Box 1190
Tiburon, CA 94920
website: www.scientificexploration.org
The SSE is a professional organization for scientists and scholars who study unusual and unexplained phenomena. It sponsors an annual meeting and publishes the quarterly *Journal of Scientific Exploration*. The society's website offers free online lectures and access to the society's free e-newsletter *The Explorer*.

For Further Reading

Books

Austin, Joanne. *ESP, Psychokinesis, and Psychics.* New York: Chelsea House, 2008.

Gibson, Marley. *The Other Side: A Teen's Guide to Ghost Hunting and the Paranormal.* Boston: Houghton Mifflin Harcourt, 2009.

Krippner, Stanley, and Harris L. Friedman, eds. *Mysterious Minds: The Neurobiology of Psychics, Mediums, and Other Extraordinary People.* Santa Barbara, CA: Praeger, 2010.

Marsh, Clint. *The Mentalist's Handbook: An Explorer's Guide to Astral, Spirit, and Psychic Worlds.* San Francisco: Red Wheel, 2008.

Mayer, Elizabeth Lloyd. *Extraordinary Knowing: Science, Skepticism, and the Inexplicable Powers of the Human Mind.* New York: Bantam, 2007.

Nickell, Joe. *Adventures in Paranormal Investigation.* Lexington: University Press of Kentucky, 2007.

Powell, Diane Hennacy. *The ESP Enigma: The Scientific Case for Psychic Phenomena.* New York: Walker, 2009.

Tart, Charles T. *The End of Materialism: How Evidence of the Paranormal Is Bringing Science and Spirit Together.* Oakland, CA: New Harbinger, 2009.

Winkowski, Mary Ann. *When Ghosts Speak: Understanding the World of Earthbound Spirits.* New York: Grand Central, 2009.

Wood, Maureen. *The Ghost Chronicles: A Medium and a Paranormal Scientist Investigate 17 True Hauntings.* Naperville, IL: Sourcebooks, 2009.

Periodicals

Begley, Sharon, Karen Springen, and Kurt Soller. "Why We Believe," *Newsweek,* November 3, 2008.

Blow, Charles M. "Paranormal Flexibility," *New York Times,* December 12, 2009.

Byrnes, Sholto. "Britain's Hidden Religion," *New Statesman*, April 13, 2009.

Clark, Jeremy. "'I'll Have Nothing to Do with No Ouija Board. No Way,'" *Spectator*, August 5, 2006.

Clark, Matthew. "Phantasms of the Living," *Antioch Review*, Winter 2010.

Fox, Douglas. "Through the Mind's Eye: Our Innermost Thoughts and Visions Might Not Be Secret for Long," *New Scientist*, May 6, 2006.

Fraser, Sylvia. "Team Spirit," *Toronto Life*, November 2007.

Grove, Sophie. "Paranormal Activities," *Newsweek International*, May 31, 2010.

Jarvis, Tim. "Twilight Zone Explained," *O, The Oprah Magazine*, December 2007.

Kester, Douglas, and Jerome S. Rovner. "Speculating on the Soul," *Discover*, August 2007.

Phillips, Helen. "Déjà Vu All Over Again: Unravel the Weird Experience of Déjà Vu and You Begin to See How We Distinguish Fantasy from Reality," *New Scientist*, March 28, 2009.

Remo, Jessica. "Spirits in the Night," *New Jersey Monthly*, October 2010.

Wise, Jeff. "This Is Your Brain . . . ," *Popular Mechanics*, November 2007.

Index

Nebuchadnezzar
(Babylonian king), 92,
93
New Age beliefs, percentage
of Americans following,
106
Novus Spiritus church, 99
Nunes, S.S., 68

O
O'Brien, Nan, 32
Old Testament
on false *vs.* true prophets,
94–95
prophecy in, 92–93
prophets of, *95*
OOBE. *See* Out-of-body
experiences
Opinion polls. *See* Surveys
Oppenheimer, Mark,
102
Oscar (cat), 8
Out-of-body experiences
(OOBE)
prevalence of, 27, 28
triggers for, *23*
virtual reality can
simulate, 21–25

P
Padre Pio, 99
Paranormal America, 62
Paranormal phenomena
are not simply
neurological disorders,
26–31

close relationship exists
between religious
experiences and,
96–101
interest in, may be a fad,
84–89
Paranormal TV shows,
ratings for, *88*
Paranormal/pseudoscience
detract from legitimate
science, 50–57, *82*
percentage of teens
having experimented
with, *82*
See also Belief in
paranormal
Parapsychological
Association, 47
Parnia, Sam, 111, 112
Paul the Octopus, 7
Penman, Danny, 108
The Pet Psychic (TV
program), 8
Pets, psychic abilities of, 7–9
Polls. *See* Surveys
Popular culture, 56
fosters belief in
paranormal, 77–83
Price, H.H., 48
Prophets
of Old Testament, *95*
Old Testament on false
vs. true, 94–95

R
Randi, James, 49

Picture Credits

AP Images, 41

The Art Archive/British Library, 104

Oscar Burriel/Photo Researchers, Inc., 17, 28

© Jack Carey/Alamy, 86

© Corbis Cusp/Alamy, 46

Gale/Cengage Learning, 23, 30, 48, 54, 63, 75, 82, 88, 95, 98, 106, 112

© Geoff A. Howard/Alamy, 61

James King-Holmes/W Industries/Photo Researchers, Inc., 24

© Lebrecht Music and Arts Photo Library/Alamy, 90, 93

© Dale O'Dell/Alamy, 58

© Oote Boe Photography 2/Alamy, 10

Christina Pedrazzini/Photo Researchers, Inc., 70

© Photo Alto/Alamy, 79

© Pollard Stock/Alamy, 110

© Robert Harding Picture Library Ltd/Alamy, 53

Scala/Art Resource, NY, 100

SPL/Photo Researchers, Inc., 76